BUILT
TO LAST

BUILT
TO LAST

How to Build Strong and Lasting Relationships
With God, Family, and Friends

Kenneth W. Hagin

18 17 16 15 14 13 12   08 07 06 05 04 03 02

Built to Last (paperback)
ISBN-13: 978-0-89276-753-3, ISBN-10: 0-89276-753-7
(formerly ISBN-13: 978-0-89276-742-7, 10: 0-89276-742-1)

Copyright © 2002, 2011 Rhema Bible Church
AKA Kenneth Hagin Ministries, Inc.
All rights reserved.
First edition 2002. Paperback edition 2011.
Printed in USA

In the U.S. write:
Kenneth Hagin Ministries
P.O. Box 50126
Tulsa, OK 74150-0126
1-888-28-FAITH
www.rhema.org

In Canada write:
Kenneth Hagin Ministries of Canada
P.O. Box 335, Station D
Etobicoke (Toronto), Ontario
Canada M9A 4X3
1-866-70-RHEMA
www.rhemacanada.org

CONTENTS

CHAPTER ONE

God Wants You!

There are various types of relationships in which we can be involved. There is the divine relationship between God and man, the marriage relationship between husband and wife, and the family relationship between relatives, just to name a few. The *kinds* of relationships we form can be just as varied. For example, there is a covenant relationship with God, as well as a covenant relationship with other people. There is a working relationship between fellow workers and between employees and employers. There is a mentoring relationship—between teacher and student, for example. And there is a believer's relationship with other believers, which includes friendships.

We're going to study these various types and kinds of relationships in the following chapters. In this chapter, we'll look at the first and most important type of relationship—the divine relationship between God and man.

If we're going to learn what God has to say about relationships, we need to start in the Book of Beginnings, with the first relationship between God and man. But first, I want to relate a story that reminds me of how God feels about mankind.

One day a little girl who had been adopted was playing with her sisters who had been born into this particular family. When one of the sisters got upset, she cruelly informed her adopted sister, "You were adopted. You don't really belong to this family."

The little adopted girl thought for a moment and then quietly answered, "Mom and Dad didn't have any choice about you. But they chose me. They have me because they chose me."

This little girl's description of how her mom and dad felt about her describes God's feelings about all mankind. He chose each of us before we were ever born. And He wants to have a relationship with us.

God created you in His image. And God wants you to be connected with Him and have a relationship with Him.

GENESIS 1:26–27 (NKJV)

26 Then God said, "Let Us make man in Our image, according to Our likeness; let them have dominion over the fish of the sea, over the birds of the air, and over the cattle, over all the earth and over every creeping thing that creeps on the earth."

27 So God created man in His [own] image; in the image of God He created him; male and female He created them.

This passage of scripture tells us that God created man in His image and likeness. God wants a relationship with the one He created. That means mankind—His creation—was designed with the desire to have a relationship with God and with others.

Relationship Defined

What exactly is a relationship? *The Scribner-Bantam English Dictionary* defines *relationship* as "connection, kinship, or involvement." Other words with a similar meaning to *relationship* are *affiliation, association,* and *belonging.* A relationship is something two or more people establish, usually by choice.

God created you to be connected to Him. All mankind was created to have a relationship with God. Although every person may not have a relationship with God at this moment, nevertheless every person was created for such a relationship.

There used to be a popular slogan that the United States Armed Forces used for recruiting. Posters displayed a picture of Uncle Sam pointing a finger and the caption read, "Uncle Sam wants *you!*"

I want you to imagine God sitting upon His throne in Heaven, pointing straight at you and saying, "I want *you!*" *God does want you!*

Many people today are looking for good, quality relationships, yet many people today are having problems in relationships. The reason they're having problems in relationships and having problems understanding relationships is that they have never established a relationship with God through Jesus Christ.

It is difficult to establish healthy relationships with other people if you haven't first established a relationship with the Creator. Remember, He created within mankind the desire to have a relationship with Him first and foremost. People who don't have a relationship with God will try all sorts of things to fill that void and meet that desire. They will worship the sun, trees, and all kinds of inanimate objects, trying to establish (or "find") a relationship that meets their God-designed need.

But only God can fill and meet that need. Remember, God is real! And when you allow Him to do so, He will walk with you and talk with you. God wants to have a relationship with *you*.

You Can Commune With God!

If you read the creation account in Genesis chapter 1, you will notice that after God created everything, He said, "It is good." And then on the seventh day, He rested.

God created the earth and every plant and creature in it. Then He created a man. The trees couldn't talk to God. The animals couldn't communicate intelligently with Him. The sea and the mountains were beautiful, but they could not have a relationship with God. Then He said, *"Let us make man in our image . . ."* (Gen. 1:26).

Not one of all the other creatures and living things God created was made in His image. But He created man in His image. Man can talk and communicate with God; man can have a relationship with Him. Man is the only creature who has a consciousness of God's existence and personality.

Dr. C.I. Scofield, editor of *The Scofield Reference Bible*, said, "Man is a personal, rational, and moral being. While God is infinite, man is finite. Nevertheless, man possesses the elements of personality similar to those of the Divine Person."

Think about that! Although we are finite beings, we were made to fellowship with God Himself!

Our Father's Image

During creation, God said, "Let us make man in our image and likeness" (Gen. 1:26). What is image? Strong's Concordance defines *image* as "resemblance, a representative figure." In other words, we resemble God, and we are His representatives on the earth. The word *likeness* means "resemblance, model, shape, and fashion."

Maybe someone has told you, "You have the likeness of your father," "You're the image of your mom," or "You look just like your sister." Wouldn't it be nice if people told you, "You look just like your Father God"?

When you have a relationship with God, His personality traits will be in you. Just as you exhibit your natural parents' personality traits, you can imitate your Heavenly Father (Eph. 5:1).

Recently, I was on the phone with someone, and the way I answered him about something made me think, *That tone of voice and phraseology was my daddy talking!* The older I get, the more I find myself doing things the way my dad does them. Why is that? Through the physical creation process, we have been created in our natural parents' image, so to speak.

We were also created in God's image and likeness. God created man in such a way that we could have and maintain a relationship with Him and so that man could represent God on the earth in His image and likeness.

Dominion Versus Possession

Notice that God did not give man the earth as a possession. Psalm 24:1 says, *"THE EARTH IS THE LORD'S, and the fulness thereof; the world, and they that dwell therein"* (KJV). God is the possessor of earth, but God did give man *dominion* over the earth to rule and subdue it through a relationship with Him.

GENESIS 1:26 (NKJV)

26 Then God said, "Let Us make man in Our image, according to Our likeness; let them have dominion over the fish of the sea, over the birds of the air, and over the cattle, over all the earth and over every creeping thing that creeps on the earth."

There is a difference between someone giving you *dominion* over something and someone giving you *possession* of something. Through our relationship with God, we have been given the dominion—the power—to rule and reign on the earth. But dominion is only possible through a relationship with Him.

Father and Child

When God created Adam, they had a perfect relationship in a perfect environment. They communicated freely and enjoyed daily fellowship. The Bible says that God came down in the *"cool of the day"* to talk with Adam (Gen. 3:8). They worked together and existed together on a relationship basis.

We, too, need to exist together with God on a relationship basis. We need to relate to Him as Friend and Father—not just as a Higher Power or Supreme Deity, even though He is both of those things.

We should exist together with God as our personal Father. He *is* a Higher Power. He *is* Supreme Deity. But we should have a relationship with Him on a personal basis, not just because He is deity, but because He is our very own Father and we are His very own children.

CHAPTER TWO

We Need Other People

In the spring of 1953, Edmund Hillary and his Nepalese guide, Tenzing Norgay, were working their way up Mount Everest in preparation for their historic assault on the summit May 29. Suddenly, Hillary lost his footing. Norgay quickly grabbed the rope that joined them and held it taut, keeping Hillary from falling.

Just as Hillary and Norgay needed to be connected to each other by a rope while climbing Mt. Everest, so every person needs relationships that connect them with others.

God not only created you to have a relationship with *Him*, He created you to have relationships with *other people*. He created us in such a way that we need others. Even though Adam had a relationship with God, it wasn't enough. God Himself said so!

GENESIS 2:18 (NKJV)

18 And the Lord God said, "It is not good that man should be alone; I will make him a helper comparable to him."

God and man had a relationship with each other, but God said it wasn't good for man to be alone. That is why He made a helper for him. It's important to understand that we need each other.

Some people want to isolate themselves and live like recluses, thinking they can make it on their own and that they don't need anyone else. But God said it's not enough for us just to have a relationship with Him; we need other people!

How can having relationships with other people benefit us? We can minister to each other and help one another. We can support and pray for each other. We need other people whether we think we do or not.

Why don't some people make an effort to establish and maintain relationships? They don't realize the importance of it. Maybe they had a bad relationship experience in the past. Maybe they have seen only bad examples of relationships.

Some people might say, "Relationships are just too hard. They require too much effort, too much time, and too much attention." Yes, building and maintaining a meaningful relationship does require all these things. But in your hour of need, you will be looking for someone to give you a helping hand. And if you haven't already established a relationship with someone, you might be left to face your situation alone.

People have said, "God is all I need." Well, if all mankind needed was God, why did God look at man, determine he needed a helper, and then create another person for him to have a relationship with?

Relationships with other people are important. They are important to God, and they should be important to us too.

A Sense of Belonging

Often people who don't have a meaningful relationship with another person experience feelings of loneliness. Without meaningful human relationships, a person may feel as though he or she doesn't belong.

Having relationships with others gives us a sense of belonging. When we have a relationship with God, we gain a sense of belonging, and when we have relationships with fellow Christians, we gain a further sense of belonging.

Have you noticed when people talk about where they attend church, some say, "I *attend* such-and-such church," while others say, "I *belong* to such-and-such church"? There's a difference. Some people go to church even though they don't have any meaningful relationships within the congregation. But the person who has built relationships will say, "*I belong. . . .*"

If someone asked you why you belong to your particular local church, you might begin to name the people with whom you have built relationships. We belong to a group or organization because we've established relationships within those groups.

Each member of my pastoral staff has a relationship with one another. We have a working relationship, and we have a personal relationship. I have personal feelings for every one of the families on my staff. If something happens to them, I feel it. If they go through a test or trial, I feel for them. Why? I've established a personal relationship with each of them. They're not just staff—they're friends!

Relationships Bring Success

The basis for all relationships is God. *God wants you!* He wants you to have a relationship with Him, and He wants you to have relationships with other people. Remember, man was created to have relationships. When relationships are broken, man is limited and crippled, so to speak.

I don't want you to be crippled and limited because of broken relationships. When you are able to maintain healthy, godly relationships, you are able to be tremendously effective for the Kingdom of God.

I can do some things on my own, and you can have some success on your own. But as we work together in covenant relationships with one another, we can turn our communities upside down for God!

The Church we read about in the Book of Acts got the reputation for turning the world upside down (Acts 17:6). It was through the strong relationships they had with fellow Christians that they were able to change the world around them.

ACTS 2:41–47

41 Those who accepted his message were baptized, and about three thousand were added to their number that day.

42 They devoted themselves to the apostles' teaching and to the fellowship, to the breaking of bread and to prayer.

43 Everyone was filled with awe, and many wonders and miraculous signs were done by the apostles.

44 All the believers were together and had everything in common.

45 Selling their possessions and goods, they gave to anyone as he had need.

46 Every day they continued to meet together in the temple courts. They broke bread in their homes and ate together with glad and sincere hearts,

47 praising God and enjoying the favor of all the people. And the Lord added to their number daily those who were being saved.

We see in verse 46 that the apostles went to church but they also fellowshipped with one another in a home or casual setting. We can also see these two categories of relationships: people entering into a new relationship with Christ (vv. 41, 47), and people having relationships with each other (vv. 42, 46). The Kingdom of God, or the Church, is designed to be relational.

Think about this. You cannot enter the Kingdom of God unless you enter into a relationship with Jesus Christ, receiving Him as Savior and Lord. And it's very hard to enter into a strong relationship with a Christian if you aren't also in a relationship with God through Jesus.

Have you noticed what happens when people stop fellowshipping closely with God? The first thing that happens is they start neglecting their relationships with other believers. They stop attending church and stop being around the people who can give them the support and the help they need to get back into close fellowship with God. We need to stay close to our Christian friends, because they will help us and encourage us to stay close to Christ.

It was through the apostles' strong relationships with God first and people second that they were "adding to their number daily." As we build and strengthen our relationship with God and with fellow Christians, we will add to our number daily those who are being saved.

As a pastor, I'm not interested in catching "fish" from someone else's pond. In other words, I don't want to add to the membership of RHEMA Bible Church by stealing members from other churches. I want our membership to increase because we are winning the lost to Jesus Christ, so they, too, can experience relationships with Him and with other Christians.

There's Strength in Numbers

Let me give you an illustration to demonstrate the strength that is found in numbers. I can take a single stick and easily snap it in two. But if I took a group of sticks (with each individual stick about the same size as the single one I snapped in two), put them all together in a bundle, bound the bundle on each end with a rawhide strip, and tried to pop the bundle of sticks over my knee, I wouldn't be able to break a single stick!

Many times, the devil or circumstances will come to us individually and snap us in half, so to speak. But if we'll bind together in a covenant relationship—bound together by the love and peace of God—the devil can come against us and rant and rave, but he won't be able to break us. He may bend us a little bit, but he can't break us! There's strength in numbers.

When people begin to see us bound together in a covenant relationship and busy helping one another through various situations, they will want to be a part of that kind of relationship. We'll get them saved and born into God's Kingdom. Our churches will be filled with new babes in Christ!

Some of these new converts may not look or act the way we do. That's all right. Too many people try to clean up the outside before they clean up the inside. But if a person has Jesus working on the

inside, it will eventually show up on the outside. When we understand godly relationships, we can shake hands with people who may
not look the way we do. We can be friendly and even offer them our
seat at church or at a social function if necessary. We Christians
need to be ready, willing, and able to help people establish and build
a relationship with God and others in the Body of Christ.

The Dangers of *Not* Having Relationships

Let's take a closer look at how relationships can help us as
believers in the Church. Churches are strong and healthy when
the people in it have strong relational ties with each other.

I want to talk about the necessity of having good relationships
and share some benefits of having healthy relationships in the
Church. But if we're going to look at relationships that can help
believers, the first thing we must do is become aware of the dangers of not having relationships.

One of the best ways to find out what something is, is to find
out what it's not. So one of the best ways to find out how relationships with fellow believers can help us is to discover the dangers
of not having relationships in the Church.

The devil wants to destroy relationships in the Church so he
can rob people of the redemptive benefits they have through
Christ. If he can rob people of relationships, he can isolate them
and more easily attack them. One danger of not having relationships in the Church is a *limited defense system to protect yourself.*

When you were a child growing up, did you have a big brother
or friend that you could count on if you got into a fight or difficult

situation? That person was part of your defense system. He helped you protect yourself against an enemy.

In the same way, the relationships you build within the Church offer you a defense system. Your brothers and sisters in Christ can help defend you against your enemy, the devil.

In the Old Testament, Elisha's servant became afraid because the enemy surrounded him.

2 KINGS 6:15–18

15 When the servant of the man of God got up and went out early the next morning, an army with horses and chariots had surrounded the city. "Oh, my lord, what shall we do?" the servant asked.

16 "Don't be afraid," the prophet answered. "Those who are with us are more than those who are with them."

17 And Elisha prayed, "O Lord, open his eyes so that he may see." Then the Lord opened the servant's eyes, and he looked and saw the hills full of horses and chariots of fire all round Elisha.

18 As the enemy came down toward him, Elisha prayed to the Lord, "Strike these people with blindness." So he struck them with blindness, as Elisha had asked.

Notice the servant ceased to be afraid when Elisha, with whom he had a relationship, said, "*Don't be afraid . . . Those who are with us are more than those who are with them*" (2 Kings 6:16). The relationship the servant had with Elisha provided him with a protection he wouldn't have known otherwise!

Limited Provision

Without strong relationships with other Christians, you have a limited defense system. You also have *limited provision for yourself.*

You are limited in what you can achieve and in what you can receive, because you are depending entirely upon yourself. When you don't have relationships with others, everything depends upon you! You can't expect anyone to help you or give to you in any way. When you have no relationships, whatever you gain depends entirely on you. You are limited by what you can supply with your own efforts.

Another danger in not having relationships is that you receive *limited or no support from others.* I'm not just talking about physical sustenance, although that is included. I'm talking about emotional, mental, and spiritual support and encouragement one to another.

I've been in the ministry more than forty-five years, and I have observed that when people haven't established relationships with other Christians, the devil has them exactly where he wants them. He has them isolated and alone. And once he has them isolated, he will give them a problem so big they can't handle it by themselves.

Resist the feeling that no one wants you around or that no one is interested in you. That is the devil talking to your mind to keep you from stepping out and developing new relationships. He is trying to isolate you so that you will lose the added protection and provision that relationships afford you.

In God's Word, we see that His people had relationships vital to their well-being and success. Moses needed Aaron and Hur. Joshua needed Caleb. Naomi needed Ruth. David needed Jonathan (who saved his life), and Jonathan needed David (to provide for his family). Paul needed Barnabas and Silas. We need each other!

Don't Leave the Herd!

If you'll study the animal kingdom, you can understand how the devil works. When a predator animal such as a wolf wants to capture a deer, he does not attack the whole herd. He works to isolate one deer (or waits for it to wander off or lag behind the others), and then he attacks it because it no longer has the protection of the herd. He won't attack the whole herd, because if he did, the herd would easily outnumber and defeat him.

The predator will often try to single a baby animal out of the herd because it will be less able to defend itself. But watching animal herds, you see that every animal in the herd, not just the mother, looks out for the young ones. And if they see a young one start to stray, they will try to corral it back into the herd. And when danger comes, the adult animals surround the younger animals to protect them from harm. The adult animals do most of the fighting.

That's the kind of relationship we need to establish in the Church. The young ones who haven't learned how to fight the fight of faith on their own need to be surrounded and protected by the mature Christians who have been through wars with the devil and have emerged victorious!

Reach Your Potential!

We've studied the dangers of not having healthy relationships. Now let's look at some of the benefits. One benefit of having healthy relationships is that they *enable us to reach our full potential.*

Let's read Ephesians 4:15 and 16.

EPHESIANS 4:15-16

15 Instead, speaking the truth in love, we will in all things grow up into him who is the Head, that is, Christ.

16 From him the whole body, joined and held together by every supporting ligament, grows and builds itself up in love, as each part does its work.

Each member of the human body depends upon the other members in order to function properly. The same is true in the Body of Christ.

There is the Church in general—the Body of Christ. And there is also the local church. The local church only functions properly as each person in the church is in relationship with one another. As each member is in his place, doing his part, and working together with other members doing their part, the will of God for that local church is accomplished and the Body of Christ at large is blessed.

It's not good for Christians to be "lone rangers." We need to work with each other and establish relationships with other believers. The husband and wife should be a team. Our family should be a team. And every church member needs to work together in relationship with one another as a team.

Notice, there are no "I's" in the word "team." An acronym for the word team is *"Together Each Achieves More."* I like that!

I shudder to think what would happen if I had to pastor RHEMA Bible Church all by myself. I can't do everything—preach, lead worship, lead children's and youth services, teach Sunday school classes, organize church socials, visit hospitals, nursing homes, and prisons, head up street evangelism, and so forth. My pastoral staff, my church leaders, and my volunteers—they're my team! And because we are a team working together, we are able to accomplish more for God, benefiting our church members, our community, and the world!

Remember, the Bible says that one man can put one thousand to flight, but two men can put ten thousand to flight (Deut. 32:30). When you join with believers, you don't just double your power, you multiply it. Imagine what five can do! Imagine what *five thousand* believers can accomplish!

Tap Into a Full Supply

A second benefit relationships provide is a *full supply for everyone*. Relationships are the connection through which we can experience the full supply of what we need!

Notice how the people in the Church in the Book of Acts shared with each other.

ACTS 2:44-45

44 All the believers were together and had everything in common.

45 Selling their possessions and goods, they gave to anyone as he had need.

When we have a need, it's usually more profitable to go to the people with whom we already have a relationship. Imagine walking up to a total stranger or knocking on the door of someone you don't know and asking for help, food, or whatever it is you need. Chances are that you won't receive the help you need from strangers.

If I needed to borrow money for something, I would go to people who know me, people with whom I already have a relationship. When I was in Bible school, I sometimes borrowed money for gas from a friend or a family member. You see, when I needed something, I went to the people who wanted to help me. (As a side note, I want you to know that I paid them back. If a friend loans you something, you need to pay them back. Otherwise, you could cause damage to the relationship, not to mention your conscience before God.)

Whether or not you're facing a financial struggle, you need others! For example, if my car were to stall, and I needed to push it to a gas station across the street, I may give it every ounce of strength and effort I have and still not be able to move it. But suppose a friend of mine came along and helped me push. We would be able to move the car a little bit. Then suppose another friend came along and joined us. And then a fourth friend added his strength. In no time at all, we would be able to push the car to the station. The job could be completed because we were in relationship, working together toward a common goal.

Let me borrow an illustration from economist Milton Friedman to further show our need for others. A pencil is a simple object. But the wood for that pencil may come from a forest in Washington. The graphite needed for the lead may come from a mine in South America. And the eraser may be obtained from a Malaysian rubber plantation. Thousands of people co-operate to make something as simple as a pencil.

Now these are simple illustrations, but think of what can happen for God when all of us in His Body establish relationships with one another and start working together for the Kingdom!

Join the Network!

A third benefit relationships provide is a *network of support.*

A "net-working" can be seen in the operation of a fishing net. Every strand is needed; without each strand, no net would exist. Every knot is necessary so that the many strands come together and do what one strand cannot—form a net around the fish to catch them. One strand by itself will not catch any fish, but many strands carefully joined together will catch many fish.

You cannot reach your full potential and accomplish the complete will of God by yourself any more than you can catch fish with one strand of rope! We must all be carefully joined together in relationships so that we can receive and wisely use all that God has for us.

What one person cannot accomplish by himself, many people joined together in relationships *can* accomplish. When all of us are in relationship with one another, we can throw out the net and be successful *fishers of men*!

I can't do what you can do, and you can't do what I can do, but together, we can accomplish anything. Relationships give us an opportunity to partner with someone else and to bring increase into our life and the lives of others.

I see this principle at work in the relationships I have with my pastoral staff. Every member of my staff has his own personality and talents. We have recognized each other's differences and strengths, which adds increase to our relationship. I can't do what they do, and they can't do what I can do, but together we can get the job done.

The complete will of God for you and the Church will be realized as we build strong, solid, committed relationships with each other. We need each other! Our relationships with one another form a lifeline that enables us to offer help to our brothers and sisters. We can offer a lifeline of support that keeps us standing tall. And together we can help each other accomplish the will of God!

A Biblical Pattern

Again, God wants to have a personal relationship with you, and He wants you to have relationships with other people.

There is a saying that no man is an island unto himself. We all need God, and we all need other people. The Bible is full of accounts of people who had special relationships with God and with one another: Adam and Eve, God and Abraham, David and Jonathan, Naomi and Ruth, Paul and Barnabas, and so forth.

The healthier our relationship with God is, the healthier our relationships with other people will be. Let's first establish and build our relationship with God, and then He will help us build and maintain meaningful relationships with others.

CHAPTER THREE

Relationships: A Top Priority for Believers

We can see the value of relationships and the importance of establishing quality relationships and friendships with God, our families, and others. But these relationships will not automatically be formed and developed without any effort on our part. No, we must take the time and make the effort to build relationships in life. We must make relationships our top priority.

Let's look in greater detail at the Apostle Paul's discourse on the importance of relationships in the Body of Christ and their interworkings within the Body.

EPHESIANS 4:11–16

11 It was he who gave some to be apostles, some to be prophets, some to be evangelists, and some to be pastors and teachers,

12 to prepare God's people for works of service, so that the body of Christ may be built up

13 until we all reach unity in the faith and in the knowledge of the Son of God and become mature, attaining to the whole measure of the fulness of Christ.

14 Then we will no longer be infants, tossed back and forth by the waves, and blown here and there by every wind of teaching and by the cunning and craftiness of men in their deceitful scheming.

15 Instead, speaking the truth in love, we will in all things grow up into him who is the Head, that is, Christ.

16 From him the whole body, joined and held together by every supporting ligament, grows and builds itself up in love, as each part does its work.

Paul compares the Church—the Body of Christ—with the physical body. Verse 16 tells us that the Body of Christ is *"held together by every supporting ligament"* and that we only grow *"as each part does its work."* Thus, relationships must be top priority for believers!

In our fast-paced world, it's a challenge to keep our priorities in the right order and to stay focused on the right things. Everything moves so quickly; sometimes it's hard to stay focused on the truly important things.

Instead of focusing on relationships, many Christians substitute other things as their top priority. Some Christians spend all their time seeking new revelation and understanding from the Word of God. Some focus solely on experiencing new power and anointing from God.

Others concentrate on following rules, regulations, and rituals. Some focus solely on trying to reach new levels of performance. Some Christians make climbing the ladder of success their top priority.

And although some Christians view going to church as a top priority, they attend just for a spiritual experience, not a relational one. Others view attending church as a top priority, but only because they consider it a duty that has to be fulfilled.

There is nothing inherently wrong with any of these viewpoints I've mentioned. However, they should not take precedence over valuing people and the need for having relationships with others. If we disregard having relationships with other people, it will be difficult to achieve any of the other things I just listed. Relationships should be our top priority, because the success of the Body of Christ depends on each part working together.

Why We Need Pastors

For a moment, I want to look at relationships in the church, specifically in the Spirit-filled Charismatic environment. Some Charismatics have been accused of being "cruise-amatics," because they do not place a very high priority on building lasting and permanent relationships with each other. For example, if they are not happy in one church, they "pack up" and go somewhere else.

It's important that we learn to have solid, healthy relationships in the church. The first step to accomplishing this is learning how to relate to the pastor and church leaders. To do this, we must realize why we need pastoral leadership.

Ephesians 4:12 says that pastors are *"to prepare God's people for works of service, so that the body of Christ may be built up."* That's the number one job of a pastor. A pastor is not to do all the works of service himself! He is to prepare *you*—individual members—so that *you* can do the job, that the Body of Christ may be built up!

The Heart of the Pastor

In relating to the pastor and church leaders, it's also important to understand the heart of the pastoral staff.

When I study for a message, I am not studying for myself. I am not studying to build myself up. When I study, I ask God to give me revelation, wisdom, and knowledge so that I can give my congregation something that will touch their hearts, bless them, and help them with what they're facing in life.

Ephesians chapter 4 talks about the heart of the pastor.

EPHESIANS 4:12-15

12 to prepare God's people for works of service, so that the body of Christ may be built up

13 until we all reach unity in the faith and in the knowledge of the Son of God and become mature, attaining to the whole measure of the fulness of Christ.

14 Then we will no longer be infants, tossed back and forth by the waves, and blown here and there by every wind of teaching and by the cunning and craftiness of men in their deceitful scheming.

15 Instead, speaking the truth in love, we will in all things grow up into him who is the Head, that is, Christ.

We can see that pastoral leadership is ordained by God to equip the church with the Word and the Spirit to do God's work (v. 12). A pastor's heart is to help people unite in faith and grow into full maturity (v. 13). The pastor has a heart to guard the flock (v. 14), and his heart is to teach people the truth of God's Word in love (v. 15).

Pastoral Leadership Is God-Ordained

In relating to the pastor and other church leaders, you must understand why you need pastoral leadership, understand the heart of the pastoral staff, and learn to view the pastoral leadership as the God-ordained leadership in the church. The Bible says we are to follow God-ordained leadership as they follow Christ (1 Cor. 11:1).

How do you do this? First, receive the anointed message they share, not as just the words of men, but as the words of God. However, you should avoid over-dependence upon or familiarity with the pastoral staff. In other words, maintain a balance by receiving from pastoral leadership and then studying the Scriptures yourself.

1 THESSALONIANS 2:13

13 And we also thank God continually because, when you received the word of God, which you heard from us, you accepted it not as the word of men, but as it actually is, the word of God, which is at work in you who believe.

Even though you need to receive the anointed message that ministers share as the word of God, you should still study the Scriptures yourself to see if what these men and women say is true. The Bereans were commended because they did this regarding Paul's teachings (Acts 17:11)!

Pastors Are People Too

You see, the pastoral leadership is anointed by God to lead, but they are still individual human beings. They are just like you in that they're endeavoring to serve God in what He's called them to do. They've just received a different assignment. They have been anointed by God to serve Him in a leadership position. You can expect the anointing to flow through the pastoral leadership, but you also have to allow them to be human!

In other words, pastors experience trials like you do. They have to ask for forgiveness when they make a mistake—just like you do. God's Word gives us plenty of examples of anointed men and women doing some very human things!

Even though people are anointed, they can still make mistakes. David was anointed to be King of Israel, but he made some serious mistakes and had to ask God's forgiveness. The Apostle Peter was called especially by God. But Peter went out and cursed the Name of Jesus and swore he had never met Him. But Peter repented, and God restored him.

My point is that just because someone is anointed to preach doesn't mean he is no longer human. Ministers are people too.

Every time I prepare to minister, I pray, "Father, I go not in my own might and my own strength to speak my own words. I go in Your might and Your anointing to speak Your Word. When I walk on that platform, I walk not in my humanity. I walk not in my own knowledge, but I walk in Your anointing and Your Presence. And, by faith, I believe Your anointing will be upon me and that the message that comes forth will be anointed, will lift this congregation, and will meet the people's needs."

That is the prayer my staff and I pray before we minister. We pray that our words will be a "word in due season" and that the anointing will be upon us as we preach. But it will help you in relating to your pastor if you remember that he is still human and that he doesn't always operate in the same anointing when he's not ministering as he does when he's standing on the platform ministering under his calling and anointing.

Relating to Other Believers

Remember, we're learning how to build solid, healthy relationships in the church. In order to accomplish this, we must not only learn how to relate to the pastor and other church leaders; it is also important to learn how to relate to fellow believers.

Let's read Ephesians 4:15 and 16 again for insight in this area.

EPHESIANS 4:15–16

15 Instead, speaking the truth in love, we will in all things grow up into him who is the Head, that is, Christ.

16 From him the whole body, joined and held together by every supporting ligament, grows and builds itself up in love, as each part does its work.

In this passage of scripture, we see three ways to relate to each other as fellow believers.

Number one, we relate to one another by walking in love toward one another with the love of God. John 13:34 says, *"A new command I give you: Love one another. As I have loved you, so you must love one another."* According to Ephesians 4:15, one way we walk in love toward one another is by speaking the truth in love.

What does it mean to walk in love with one another? The following acrostic for the word "love" is an easy reminder of what it means to walk in love:

L—We must be *loyal* to each other.

O—We must *offer* help to each other.

V—We must *vocalize* appreciation to each other.

E—We must *encourage* each other.

Now when you think of love and you say you love your fellow Christians, I want you to ask yourself these questions: Am I being loyal to them? Am I offering help to them? Am I vocalizing my appreciation of them? Am I encouraging them?

We Are One Body

We're looking at three ways to relate to each other as fellow believers. Number one, we relate to one another by *walking in love toward one another with the love of God*. Number two, we relate to each other by necessity *because we need each other*.

The local church was meant to be a joint effort of many people worshipping God and sharing the Good News of Jesus Christ. Ephesians 4:16 says, *"From him the whole body, joined and held together by every supporting ligament, grows and builds itself up in love, as each part does its work."*

As each one of us moves into our position in the Body of Christ and does what we're supposed to do, then the whole Body matures and grows. Just as the physical body grows and matures as each part does what it's supposed to do, so we grow and mature as we, the Body, do what the Head tells us to do. Who is the Head of the Church? Jesus Christ!

Jesus tells us what our place is and what we are to do. And as each one of us does our job, it helps open the way for someone else to do his job. Why? We are all joined together!

In the natural, my hand can't grasp anything until my arm reaches for it. Every ligament is joined together. Sometimes in the Body of Christ, the "hand" can't do what it's supposed to do because the "arm" isn't doing what it's supposed to do. What one member of the Body does affects another. The way you live your life may not only keep you from accomplishing what God wants you to accomplish; it may also hinder someone else from doing what God wants him to do.

Because we are jointly fitted together, if every person is in his place doing his part, the Church will grow and build itself in love.

Join the Network and Be a Part of the Big Picture

In learning to relate to fellow believers, we've seen that we must *walk in love toward one another with the love of God* and that we do so of necessity *because we need each other.* Number three, we relate to each other *by networking with each other.*

EPHESIANS 4:16

16 . . . the whole body . . . grows and builds itself up in love, as each part does its work.

The following acrostic for the word "network" helps remind us what a network of friends helps us to do.

N—We *nurture* each other.

E—We *encourage* each other.

T—We *trust* in each other.

W—We *work* together with each other.

O—We *optimize* each other.

R—We *reach* out to each other.

K—We *know* about each other.

31

As a network of friends, we take interest in each other and look out for each other.

If you usually sit in the same area at church every time you attend, you can build a network with the people who sit around you. And if they happen to be absent a couple of times, you should be interested enough in them to check on them and see if they need encouragement or some nurturing.

A friend of yours may become weary in well-doing. Maybe something happened in his life that depleted his strength, and he needs some nurturing. That's what the Body of Christ is for—to build each other up!

Corporate Power

It's important for us to realize that God has divine connections for every one of His people, and those connections come about as we build relationships.

We also need to realize that there is a supply of the Spirit that is available to every person in the Body of Christ, since we are all connected to the Head, Who is Christ!

Each of us has a supply of the Spirit, but when we all come together in unity and faith, how much more powerful are we than one single power unit by itself! Through a relationship with Jesus and your fellow believers, you will be able to accomplish the full potential that God put within you. God designed relationships as a way to bring increase to you and to the local church.

United We Stand

I once read a book that talked about the Special Forces, the Rangers, the Foreign Legion, the English Commandos, and so forth. I read about how everyone in a particular unit had a relationship with each other and how they had to depend on and trust each other to accomplish their mission.

The book talked about one member of a team who had been injured in a battle. Even though he was injured, when he heard that his company was being sent on a special mission, he escaped from the hospital to go on the mission with his unit.

On that mission, he was wounded again. When he returned, he was asked why he did what he did. He said, "After you live and work with people, you soon realize that your survival depends upon them."[1]

As I read that, I thought, *If we Christians understood the fact that our fellow believers depend on us for their success and well-being, we might live our lives differently!*

Think about this. What the person sitting next to you at church receives from the service depends in part upon you! They need you to help them, to encourage them, and to join your faith and your love with them.

Increase Your Efforts!

A football team may have great individual players and coaches. But that team will not do as well as a similar team on which the members are watching out for each other and working for the good of their teammates.

Relationships are all about joining together—not only for our own benefit, but also for the benefit of others. We can increase our efforts as we work together. One individual can do a little bit, but as we work together in relationship, we can do a whole lot more!

The Bible says that one can put one thousand to flight, but two can put ten thousand to flight (Deut. 32:30). When you join with believers, you don't just double your power—you multiply it and optimize the power to the maximum!

Relationships are a top need for believers. Therefore, relationships should be a top priority. Determine in your heart today that you're going to establish strong relationships with other Christians. Those relationships will bring divine connections your way. They will bring a supply of the Spirit to you. Relationships will enable you to reach your full potential—individually and corporately as a church body. Relationships will bring increase to you and to the Body of Christ.

If you need to make some adjustments in your priorities, do it today. Make a decision that from now on, relationships will be a top priority for you.

---

[1] Taken from *The Pastor's Playbook* by Stan Toler and Larry Gilbert. Copyright © 2000 by Beacon Hill Press of Kansas City. All rights reserved. Used by permission of the publisher.

CHAPTER FOUR

Elements of a Healthy Relationship

We've seen from the previous chapters that God made each of us with the desire and ability to have a personal relationship with Him. We've also learned that God wants us to have healthy relationships with other people.

Before we take a closer look at the kinds of relationships we can have with other people, let's discover what the Bible says about relationships as we examine the elements of a healthy relationship.

1 CORINTHIANS 12:13–18 (NKJV)

13 For by one Spirit we were all baptized into one body—whether Jews or Greeks, whether slaves or free—and have all been made to drink into one Spirit.

14 For in fact the body is not one member but many.

15 If the foot should say, "Because I am not a hand, I am not of the body," is it therefore not of the body?

16 And if the ear should say, "Because I am not an eye, I am not of the body," is it therefore not of the body?

17 If the whole body were an eye, where would be the hearing? If the whole were hearing, where would be the smelling?

18 But now God has set the members, each one of them, in the body just as He pleased.

From our text in First Corinthians chapter 12, we can see that everyone is important to God. First, everyone is important because God loves us all. Second, we are all important to God because Jesus Christ died on the Cross of Calvary for our salvation. Third, we are all important to God because we don't have the ability to live life completely alone—just by our own individual talents and gifts. We all have different gifts and abilities that can help others, and we need each other's strengths and talents.

I like using the following acrostic for the word "relationships" to show the elements that are necessary for building and maintaining healthy relationships.

R—*Reaching* out to others

E—*Enjoying* each other

L—*Loyal* to each other

A—*Available* to each other

T—*Trusting* of each other

I—*Interested* in each other

O—*Open* with each other

N—*Needing* each other

S—*Supporting* each other

H—*Helping* each other

I—*Investing* in each other

P—*Praying* for each other

S—*Strengthening* each other

I want you to see what a relationship really consists of. And I want you to understand that each one of these letters stands for an element that must be present if the relationship is to be a healthy one.

Reaching Out to Others

The first element is represented by the letter "R" which stands for *reaching out to others*. God has already reached out to us through His Son Jesus. And we saw in Chapter 1 the necessity of our relationship with God through Jesus Christ.

We see in the Word of God how Jesus reached out to Peter after Peter had denied Him three times.

JOHN 21:15-19

15 When they had finished eating, Jesus said to Simon Peter, "Simon son of John, do you truly love me more than these?" "Yes, Lord," he said, "you know that I love you." Jesus said, "Feed my lambs."

16 Again Jesus said, "Simon son of John, do you truly love me?" He answered, "Yes, Lord, you know that I love you." Jesus said, "Take care of my sheep."

17 The third time he said to him, "Simon son of John, do you love me?" Peter was hurt because Jesus asked him the third time, "Do you love me?" He said, "Lord, you know all things; you know that I love you." Jesus said, "Feed my sheep.

18 I tell you the truth, when you were younger you dressed yourself and went where you wanted; but when you are old you will stretch out your hands, and someone else will dress you and lead you where you do not want to go."

19 Jesus said this to indicate the kind of death by which Peter would glorify God. Then he said to him, "Follow me!"

Jesus demonstrated four things to Peter in this passage of scripture. First, Jesus focused on the love God had for Peter. Second, Jesus reminded Peter three times of the call of God upon his life.

Third, Jesus restored the relationship between Peter and Himself. (Peter had denied knowing Jesus three times after Jesus was betrayed.) And, fourth, Jesus enabled Peter to have a relationship with Him once again.

Peter was part of Jesus' inner circle. There were twelve disciples, but Peter, James, and John had a different kind of relationship with the Master. (You see, there are many different kinds of relationships. There can be acquaintances, close friends, best friends, and so forth.) Peter was a close friend of Jesus, but on the night Jesus was betrayed, he denied he knew Him.

Even so, Jesus understood the importance of relationships, and He reached out to Peter. If we're going to have healthy relationships, we're going to have to reach out to others.

Many people want to have relationships with others, but they're not willing to reach out. They're not willing to extend themselves. And there can be no relationship until you're willing to extend yourself and make the effort to build a relationship.

God extended Himself to us by giving His Son Jesus, who died on the Cross. God reached out to us. And if we're going to have a relationship with Him, we have to reach out to Him in return by receiving the gift of His Son. A relationship is a two-way street and requires both parties to reach out.

Enjoying Each Other

The first element of a healthy relationship is reaching out to others. The second element is *enjoying each other*. Proverbs 17:22 says, *"A merry heart doeth good like a medicine: but a broken spirit drieth the bones"* (KJV).

Never underestimate the value of having fun with one another— with your friends, with your spouse, with your children. Having fun and laughing together are signs of a healthy relationship.

How long has it been since you've had a good laugh with your spouse, with your friends, or with your family?

Victor Borge, an internationally renowned pianist and humorist, said, "Laughter is the shortest distance between two people." And Richard Baxter, a seventeenth-century English minister and author, said, "Keep company with the more cheerful sort of the godly; there is no mirth like the mirth of believers."[1]

Merriam-Webster's Collegiate Dictionary, Tenth Edition, defines *mirth* as "gladness or gaiety as shown by or accompanied with laughter." There is no laughter like the laughter of believers, for we truly have a reason to rejoice and be glad. We don't have to have something to pump us up! We don't have to take a pill or drink something. We've already had a drink of the Holy Spirit; we've already had a drink from the spring of Living Water!

Loyal to Each Other

So we know that the first element of a healthy relationship is reaching out to others. The second element is enjoying each other. And the third element is loyalty. In a healthy relationship, it is vitally important that you be *loyal to each other.* There can be no friendship relationship without this element. You can't be a true friend if you don't know how to be loyal.

Someone might say, "I just can't find any friends." Are you doing what the Word says? Proverbs 18:24 says, *"A man who has friends must himself be friendly, But there is a friend who sticks closer than a brother"* (NKJV). The Bible tells us that in order to have friends, we must show ourselves friendly.

If you want friends, are you showing yourself friendly? Are you reaching out to others? Are you a person upon whom people can depend?

Loyalty is one quality of a faithful person. A loyal friend is dependable—someone you can trust and count upon. And trust is a key part of any relationship.

Do your family members and friends have confidence in you? Are you so loyal that someone can tell you something and that's as far as it goes? If you're going to have a successful relationship, when someone tells you something in confidence, it should go no further. Your ability to keep a confidence is a mark of your loyalty.

Some people are loyal as long as it's convenient for them. But that's not true loyalty. You can't have a strong relationship with anyone if you aren't willing to be loyal.

Available to Each Other

The fourth element of a healthy relationship is being *available to each other.*

Do you maintain your relationships by the motto "Out of sight, out of mind"? In other words, as long as your friends are in sight, you have a relationship with them, but when your friends aren't around, you don't ever think about them.

Being available in your relationships involves being there when you're needed.

In your relationship with God, He is always there when you need Him. But are you there when He needs you? Can He depend upon you? When He asks you to witness to someone, are you available?

In your relationship with other people, are you available? When you have other things you need to do and a friend asks to talk to you about something important, are you available? Can people put their confidence in you?

Proverbs 25:19 says, *"Confidence in an unfaithful man in time of trouble is like a bad tooth and a foot out of joint"* (NKJV). The Bible compares having confidence in an unfaithful person in the time of trouble to having a bad tooth! What do you do with a bad tooth? You either get help for it or you get rid of it! We need to examine our relationships and determine to be a faithful friend who's available to our friends.

Availability to each other is a vital element to building and maintaining relationships.

Trusting of Each Other

The fifth element is *being trusting of each other.*

Trust has to be earned and it takes time to earn it. That's why relationships take time to build. Houses aren't built in a day, and neither are strong relationships. You can't just say, "House be built," and have it just appear for you to live in. Similarly, you can't go out one day and say, "I have a relationship with So-and-so" and expect to have a meaningful relationship with that person. No, lasting relationships are built over a period of time.

After we accept Jesus Christ as our personal Savior and are born again, we still have to build a relationship with Him. If we're going to accomplish what God wants us to accomplish, and if we're going to be the kind of friend that we need to be, we must spend time every day building our relationship with God. Then we should start building our relationships with other people.

George Eliot, a Victorian writer and humane freethinker, once said, "No soul is desolate as long as there is a human being for whom it can feel trust and reverence." If you've ever had your trust broken by someone, you've probably felt alone and deserted.

We need to be the kind of friends that people can trust. Can people say about you, "You can trust him. If he said it, he'll do it"?

Trust can also be built or broken down in business relationships or between a church and the community. For example, RHEMA Bible Church has built a good reputation with the city of Broken Arrow. It's taken years to build that trust—years of proving that our word is good. But today, our city officials know that if "RHEMA said it, they'll do it."

When we first moved the ministry to Broken Arrow in 1976, I had a meeting with our city officials, and I showed them a plot of the land we purchased, blueprints for our buildings, and so forth. I wanted to show my eagerness to cooperate with the city's codes and guidelines and to build a mutual relationship of trust. They didn't know us, but we did everything we said we were going to do, and the city began to trust us. Today, if we say we're going to do something, they know we're going to accomplish it, and they simply ask us when it's going to be done.

Can people trust you? If you say you're going to do something, can people count on you to get it done? Trustworthiness is a vital element of healthy relationships.

Interested in Each Other

In review, the first element of a healthy relationship is reaching out to others. The second element is enjoying each other. The third element is loyalty. The fourth element of a healthy relationship is being available to each other. The fifth element is trusting each other. The sixth element to building a strong relationship is showing interest. You can't have a relationship unless you're truly *interested in each other.*

If you want to establish a relationship with another person, instead of trying to get that person interested in you, become interested in him or her! (That piece of advice may help some singles!)

Sometimes the best thing we can do for another person is to give that person our undivided attention. All of us have to work at giving our full attention because we're so busy. Sometimes when people talk to us, we don't really hear what they're saying because we're busy thinking about something else. We're not really interested in listening to them.

Are you genuinely interested in other people? You will never accomplish God's plan for your life if you're not interested in the lives of other people. You can never be what you are supposed to be if you're not genuinely interested in the lives of your family, friends, and fellow believers.

The church you belong to won't be successful unless you are interested in the people who sit next to you, in front of you, and behind you. The church won't be what it's supposed to be unless the pastoral staff is interested in you, and you are interested in the pastoral staff.

If you haven't seen someone at church for a couple of Sundays, are you interested enough in that person to find out why he hasn't been there? Maybe you don't even know the person, but you know he hasn't been at Church because you usually sit near each other. You may have to work a little bit to check on him. You may have to ask one of the ushers or another church member. But if you're truly interested, you'll take the time to find out if that person is sick and needs prayer, has some other pressing need, or just needs someone to minister to him.

Taking an interest in other people is one way to build and maintain relationships. And when you sow interest, you will reap the reward of having people take an interest in you.

Open With Each Other

The seventh element requires that you be *open with each other.* Having a meaningful relationship with someone requires taking a risk. You can't have a relationship if you're not open. And being open with someone means you may be vulnerable to him or her as well. There is a degree of vulnerability in every good relationship you begin, but it's worth the risk.

If you're going to have a genuine relationship, you have to be real; you have to be true. There can be no facades or hypocrisy in the relationship if it is to succeed.

Too many people put up a false front even when trying to establish a relationship with God. It doesn't work with God, and it won't work in relationships with people, either.

Cicero said, "Friendship by its nature admits of no feigning, no pretense: as far as it goes it is both genuine and spontaneous." We must learn to be real and open with ourselves, with God, and with each other.

Needing Each Other

The letter "N" in the word "relationships" stands for *needing each other* and represents the eighth element of a healthy relationship. John Donne, a British metaphysical poet, said that no man is an island. That means that no one is complete in himself. We all need each other.

One of the greatest privileges in life is teaming up with other people to accomplish the will of God. But a team won't be successful if each person can't trust and depend on the other. If we don't have relationships with one another, the team won't be successful, and the will of God will not be accomplished.

We need each other to get the job done. And we need relationships that are trustworthy and dependable. As we each do our part to accomplish our goals and as we help others to accomplish their goals, we will be successful in accomplishing the will of God. As Mother Teresa once said, "What I can do, you cannot. What you can do, I cannot. But together we can do something beautiful for God."

Being a Team Player

We saw at the beginning of this chapter that the Body of Christ is made up of many parts that work together to achieve a common purpose.

1 CORINTHIANS 12:13–18 (NKJV)

13 For by one Spirit we were all baptized into one body—whether Jews or Greeks, whether slaves or free—and have all been made to drink into one Spirit.

14 For in fact the body is not one member but many.

15 If the foot should say, "Because I am not a hand, I am not of the body," is it therefore not of the body?

16 And if the ear should say, "Because I am not an eye, I am not of the body," is it therefore not of the body?

17 If the whole body were an eye, where would be the hearing? If the whole were hearing, where would be the smelling?

18 But now God has set the members, each one of them, in the body just as He pleased.

This passage of scripture tells us that the eye shouldn't be upset because it's not the ear, and the ear shouldn't be upset because it's not the eye. The foot shouldn't be upset because it's not the hand, and the hand shouldn't be upset because it's not the foot. Each part of the human body depends upon the other. Each part is important in its place and function.

In the Body of Christ, each part is important! We serve in different places and functions, but each of us has a part to fill. And we need each other! Relationships are a vital part of the overall health of the Body.

In a basketball game, only one person may receive the glory for scoring the points, but if he didn't have the other four players on the team helping him, he wouldn't score at all! He can't score if someone doesn't pass him the ball or help him get the open shot.

Just as the hands of every team member are needed to put the ball through the basket, so are many hands needed to help us in our daily walk with God. We need a relationship with God, but we also need relationships with other people.

Supporting Each Other

The "S" in "relationships" stands for *supporting each other.*

Galatians 6:2 and 3 says, *"Share each other's troubles and problems, and so obey our Lord's command. If anyone thinks he is too great to stoop to this, he is fooling himself. He is really a nobody"* (TLB).

We need to support our fellow Christians when they face troubles and problems. And we need *their* support when *we're* facing a negative situation.

Some "religious" people might say, "Well, I believed God for such-and-such. If *you* had any faith, you could believe God for it too."

I wish people who think that way would read Galatians 6:2 and 3. The Bible tells us to *share* one another's troubles and problems. Anyone who thinks he's too good to do this is fooling himself— he's really a no one!

We're to help people in times of trouble, and we're to help other people succeed. It's been said that every person's crowning moment happened because of great support from other people.

A few years ago, I was invited to attend a Presidential Luncheon in Washington, D.C. At the luncheon, I couldn't walk three feet without people stopping me to say something to me. I was even recognized from the platform and asked to stand in that room full of prominent people.

During the luncheon, I thought to myself, *I couldn't be here if it weren't for my church members. They have made me the pastor I am.* I stood in awe that day, realizing that I received the invitation because of my relationship with the people of RHEMA Bible Church. When I receive glory, they receive glory, because we're in relationship with one another.

There may be a "star player" on every team, but if the team is successful, it's because that star player has supportive teammates, a supportive coaching staff, and parents or mentors who supported him throughout his life. Without all of those people, he wouldn't be who he is.

Without each other in the Body of Christ, we wouldn't be who we are. We are a support to one another. We lift each other up and help one another become who God intended us to be.

Helping Each Other

The letter "H" stands for *helping each other* and represents the tenth element of a healthy relationship.

Everyone will need someone else's help at one time or another. The great basketball coach John Wooden guided UCLA to ten national championships. One of his mottoes is, "Every day, try to help someone who can't reciprocate your kindness."

Sometimes we do kind deeds for people because we want something in return. We need to help people who aren't able to reciprocate, or return, our kindness.

LUKE 6:32–36

32 [Jesus said,] "If you love those who love you, what credit is that to you? Even 'sinners' love those who love them.

33 And if you do good to those who are good to you, what credit is that to you? Even 'sinners' do that.

34 And if you lend to those from whom you expect repayment, what credit is that to you? Even 'sinners' lend to 'sinners', expecting to be repaid in full.

35 But love your enemies, do good to them, and lend to them without expecting to get anything back. Then your reward will be great, and you will be sons of the Most High, because he is kind to the ungrateful and wicked.

36 Be merciful, just as your Father is merciful."

We are to be kind to people and help people, expecting nothing in return.

This characteristic of helping others was illustrated beautifully by a member of our congregation recently. He was believing God for money for his own family, but felt impressed to invite a couple he had just met at church to have lunch with his family. This man and his wife took the visitors out to eat, intending to pay for their meal. But while they were all sitting there in the restaurant, someone else at the restaurant paid the entire bill!

When you start giving to others and helping those who can't reciprocate, guess what happens? Blessings start to come back to you! Why? *God rewards you!*

If we want to build and maintain strong relationships, it's important that we help other people. It's vital that we show kindness to others, even when we don't receive anything in return.

Investing in Each Other

The "I" in the word "relationships" stands for *investing in each other.*

It's been said, "Friendship is like a bank account. You can't continue to draw on it without making deposits."[1] The happiest moments of my life have not been when I *received* something, but when I *gave* something—when I invested in someone else's life.

I remember once when I was on the road preaching, I slipped some money in a minister's pocket without him knowing I did it. I learned later from the pastor of that particular church that the man had absolutely no money at the time and was facing some difficult circumstances. To this day, he doesn't know that I slipped him that money. But that was one of the greatest joys of my life—giving to him and helping him in his time of need.

There have been several times when my wife or I have slipped money into a person's purse or Bible. We enjoy helping and investing in other people.

If we want to experience healthy relationships, we are going to have to spend time investing in each other. Remember, the happiest you will be is when you are making a quality investment in the life of someone else.

Praying for Each Other

The first element of a healthy relationship is reaching out to others, the second is enjoying each other, the third is loyalty, and the fourth element of a healthy relationship is being available to each other. The fifth element is trusting each other, the sixth in building a strong relationship is interest, and the seventh element requires that you be open with each other.

The letter "N" in the word "relationships" stands for needing each other, the "S" stands for supporting each other, the letter "H" stands for helping each other, and the "I" stands for investing in each other. The letter "P" stands for *praying for each other,* which is the twelfth element of a healthy relationship.

The Bible has something to say about prayer in the context of relationships.

EPHESIANS 6:18

18 And pray in the Spirit on all occasions with all kinds of prayers and requests. With this in mind, be alert and always keep on praying for all the saints.

COLOSSIANS 4:12 (NCV)

12 Epaphras, a servant of Jesus Christ from your group, also greets you. He always prays for you that you will grow to be spiritually mature and have everything God wants for you.

From these scriptures we see that praying for one another is vitally important in our relationships. We're to spend time praying for our brothers and sisters in the Lord, with all kinds of prayer and requests (Eph. 6:18). And we're to pray that our fellow believers grow to be spiritually mature and have everything God wants them to have (Col. 4:12).

Strengthening Each Other

The last "S" in the word "relationships" stands for *strengthening each other.*

The Bible tells us that two are stronger than one. Relationships provide us the added strength we need in our times of struggle or weakness.

ECCLESIASTES 4:9-12

9 Two are better than one, because they have a good return for their work:

10 If one falls down, his friend can help him up. But pity the man who falls and has no one to help him up!

11 Also, if two lie down together, they will keep warm. But how can one keep warm alone?

12 Though one may be overpowered, two can defend themselves. A cord of three strands is not quickly broken.

This passage of scripture tells us that a cord of three strands is not quickly, or easily, broken. Remember the illustration I used to prove there is strength in numbers? One stick is easily broken but a group of sticks bound together is not.

When we bind together in relationships, we *multiply* our results instead of *adding* them. There's more dividend in multiplying than in adding! And when we bind together in relationships, we're going to multiply our success in fulfilling our vision. Together, we can accomplish more for God!

Do You Need a Lifeline?

Relationships are the lifeline of the believer, beginning with a relationship with Jesus Christ. Without a relationship with Jesus, no one has salvation. That is the first and primary relationship everyone should have.

If you don't have a relationship with Jesus Christ, you're not even saved. You're not even born again. The most important relationship you can have is one with Jesus Christ. If you haven't already done so, invite Him into your heart today and make Him the Lord and Savior of your life.

As we saw in Chapter 1, once you have a proper relationship with God through Jesus, you can establish proper relationships with other people. Without a proper relationship with God and others, you will be limited in life. Concentrate on building relationships—first, a relationship with the Father and Jesus Christ, and, second, a relationship with fellow Christians.

Relationships are vitally important to our maturity as believers. *Reaching* out to others; *enjoying* people; being *loyal* and *available* to each other; *trusting* each other; being *interested* in and *open* with one another; *needing, supporting,* and *helping* each other; *investing* in; *praying* for; and *strengthening* one another are what healthy relationships are all about.

---

[1]Taken from *Friendship, Love, & Laughter* by Bob Phillips. Copyright © 1993 by Harvest House Publishers, Eugene, OR 97402. Used by permission.

CHAPTER FIVE

The Marriage Relationship

I believe the Body of Christ is only as strong as each individual member's relationship with God, and each member's relationship with his or her spouse and family.

We've seen in previous chapters the importance of a relationship with God, and we've examined the elements of healthy relationships. When talking about relationships, it's also important that we study the marriage relationship.

I believe if marriage relationships are strong, the family will be strong. And if families are strong, the Church will be strong. So let's see what the Bible has to say about the marriage relationship. We'll start with one of the most famous marriages and learn a few lessons from Adam and Eve.

GENESIS 2:18–24

18 The Lord God said, "It is not good for the man to be alone. I will make a helper suitable for him."

19 Now the Lord God had formed out of the ground all the beasts of the field and all the birds of the air. He brought them to the man to see

what he would name them; and whatever the man called each living creature, that was its name.

20 So the man gave names to all the livestock, the birds of the air and all the beasts of the field. But for Adam no suitable helper was found.

21 So the Lord God caused the man to fall into a deep sleep; and while he was sleeping, he took one of the man's ribs and closed up the place with flesh.

22 Then the Lord God made a woman from the rib he had taken out of the man, and he brought her to the man.

23 The man said, "This is now bone of my bones and flesh of my flesh; she shall be called 'woman', for she was taken out of man."

24 For this reason a man will leave his father and mother and be united to his wife, and they will become one flesh.

From this passage of scripture, we see that God originally created man with the ability and the need for relationships. First, man had a relationship with God Himself. And God said that wasn't enough for man. Man was also designed to have a marriage relationship.

Notice verse 24 doesn't use the word "partner." It says that man shall leave his father and mother and be united to his *wife*! That means God designed for man to have a marriage relationship with a *woman*. God did not create "Adam and Steve" or "Eve and Louise"! He put Adam and Eve together—male and female; that is the biblical way.

Before I go further into studying the marriage relationship, let me say that if you choose to be single, that is your choice. You have that right and you have nothing to be ashamed of. For most people, it is God's best for them to be married. However, the important thing is to follow God's plan for *your* life.

For our study, I want to look at the latter portion of Genesis 2:18 in several different translations.

"I will make him a helper as his partner."

—New Revised Standard Version

"I will make a helper who is right for him."

—New Century Version

"I will make a companion who will help him."

—New Living Translation

"I will make him a suitable helper, completing him."

—The Berkeley Translation

"I will make him a helper meet (suitable, adapted, complementary) for him."

—Amplified Bible

Notice again that God created man and put him in the Garden. Man had a perfect relationship with God in which he fellowshipped with God. Man had a perfect environment in the Garden of Eden. His every material need was supplied. He was secure and protected. And in the midst of this perfect situation, God said, "It's not good," and created woman to be his helper. God created woman to dwell alongside man and be his companion, partner, and counterpart.

In the midst of his perfect environment, Adam needed help. And if most men today who are married will admit it, they would be in big trouble without their wives. Have you ever heard a husband refer to his wife as his "better half"? I gladly admit that I might look like a clown when I dress if it wasn't for my wife. She coordinates my colors and my clothes for me and helps me in every area of life.

What Is Marriage?

What is marriage? Some people describe marriage as the "coexistence of two people." Some say it is a covenant between two people. Others say it is merely the formal result of two people being in love. Let me tickle your funny bone a little bit with some humorous sayings about marriage.

- Marriage is like twirling a baton, or turning a cartwheel, or eating with chopsticks—it looks so easy until you try it.

- Marriage is like a violin—after the music stops, the strings are still attached.

- Marriage is the alliance of two people: one who never forgets a birthday, and the other who never remembers a birthday.[1]

- It's been said that Adam and Eve had an ideal marriage because Adam didn't have to hear about all the men that Eve could have married, and Eve didn't have to hear how good Adam's mother could cook!

These are just humorous sayings to make us laugh, but many people would probably say they can relate to these descriptions of marriage. I believe these observations fall far short of what God intended the marriage relationship to be. God intended marriage to be an institution based upon mutual respect and a healthy relationship that a man and a woman have developed with each other.

Marriage Lessons From Adam and Eve

We can learn some things about the marriage relationship if we'll study the account of Adam and Eve and see how they related to each other as husband and wife.

One area in which we can gain knowledge from Adam and Eve is the area of communication. Adam and Eve didn't communicate effectively with one another. Eve didn't bother to talk to Adam before she ate the forbidden fruit. She didn't talk to Adam and ask what he thought about Satan's ideas and suggestions concerning God's command.

Adam wasn't responsible to communicate to Eve when she was tempted. He didn't tell her, "No, don't eat of the tree. Let's obey God." Adam obviously didn't communicate much with Eve when she gave him the fruit, because he ate it too!

If you're going to have a good marriage relationship, *communication with each other* must be of the highest priority—both verbal and non-verbal communication.

What is non-verbal communication? Well, if you're a husband, you may know what it's like to get a kick in the leg under the dinner table if you're saying something you're not supposed to. That's *non-verbal* communication! Your wife is telling you to be quiet because you're telling too much information!

And for any husband who doesn't know about "the kick," I'm sure you know about "the look." You may not know what you've said or what you've done, but when you get that look, you know you've crossed the line!

These are humorous illustrations of some of the ways we communicate with our spouses. But on a serious note, open and loving communication is the key to a healthy marriage relationship.

I'm being honest with you about real marital issues. If we are to succeed in our relationship with our spouse, we need to learn to communicate properly with our mate and then bind together to protect our union against anything that comes against it. Communication is vitally important if we're going to have a proper marriage relationship. Eve allowed Satan's words to persuade her to do something that she shouldn't have done. And she didn't consult with her husband before she did it.

God gave us our spouse to help us make decisions and give us godly counsel. Adam and Eve should have communicated better with each other. And if we're to learn from their mistakes, we need to learn how to effectively communicate with *our* spouse.

Protect Your Marriage

The account of Adam and Eve teaches us that we need good communication with our spouse. Another thing we can learn is the importance of guarding our affections and keeping them directed toward our spouse and not someone else. We can also learn how to guard our spouse from someone else's affections.

There may be people who try to entice you or your spouse, but if you have good communication, you can talk to each another about it and handle the situation together.

No matter where we are in public, whether my wife and I are standing together or apart, she always has her eyes on me; she is aware of where I am in the room. And I'm glad. If she sees another woman doing something unusual or improper, she comes over and stands between the other woman and me and asks her, "May I help you?"

It sends a silent message, saying, "If you want to mess with my husband, you have to go through me. And I don't think that's going to happen."

Don't Pass the Buck!

Another lesson we can learn from Adam and Eve is in the area of blame-shifting. It will help our marriage relationship greatly if when we make a mistake, we admit it and take responsibility for our own mistakes.

When God asked Adam if he had eaten from the tree, Adam told God, "It's not my fault. It's my wife's fault. It was the woman You gave me" (Gen. 3:12). But it was Adam's own fault! He didn't *have* to eat from that tree!

Adam blamed Eve for getting them kicked out of the Garden, and Eve might have resented Adam for blaming her. But I really believe that if they had communicated properly with one another, they would have come up with a better idea than the one they ended up with (eating the fruit and then blame-shifting).

But Adam and Eve didn't communicate with one another; they did their own thing. And that's one problem with marriages today—people are doing their own thing. In today's world, a lot of houses aren't homes. They are "hotels" where family members drop by, get a little sleep, grab something to eat, and take off again. The only communication they have is "Hello," "Hope you had a good day," and "Good-bye."

Is your house a home or a hotel? Do your family members pass one another as they're going to their cars? Do you have a house, cars, and clothes, but no communication?

Just because you live with someone doesn't mean you are automatically going to have a good relationship with that person. If you're going to have a relationship with someone, you have to work on it. If you're going to have a relationship with someone, you have to get to know that person over a period of time.

God's Instructions for Marriage

In the Word of God, we find instructions given for the marriage relationship. If people would just follow these simple instructions, we wouldn't have the problems we see in marriages today.

EPHESIANS 5:21–33

21 Submit to one another out of reverence for Christ.

22 Wives, submit to your husbands as to the Lord.

23 For the husband is the head of the wife as Christ is the head of the church, his body, of which he is the Savior.

24 Now as the church submits to Christ, so also wives should submit to their husbands in everything.

25 Husbands, love your wives, just as Christ loved the church and gave himself up for her

26 to make her holy, cleansing her by the washing with water through the word,

27 and to present her to himself as a radiant church, without stain or wrinkle or any other blemish, but holy and blameless.

28 In this same way, husbands ought to love their wives as their own bodies. He who loves his wife loves himself.

29 After all, no one ever hated his own body, but he feeds and cares for it, just as Christ does the church—

30 for we are members of his body.

31 "For this reason a man will leave his father and mother and be united to his wife, and the two will become one flesh."

32 This is a profound mystery—but I am talking about Christ and the church.

33 However, each one of you also must love his wife as he loves himself, and the wife must respect her husband.

From this passage of scripture, we begin to see the proper marriage relationship—one in which both husband and wife are submitted to God and each other.

It's true that the wife is to submit, or give respect, to her own husband as the Church is submitted to Christ. It is also true that the husband is to love his wife as Christ loved the Church. How much does Christ love the Church? Christ loved the Church so much that He gave His life for it.

In the marriage relationship, there must be a head or leader. My father has always said that anything with two heads is a freak. In other words, it's not normal for there to be two leaders in a family relationship. In the church, in the workplace, and at home, someone has to be the leader. The Word of God has designated the man, the husband, to be the leader of the marriage relationship and the family.

The reason that wives sometimes take over and become the spiritual head of the house is because the husband will not do his duty according to the Word of God. I'm not saying that the husband is to dominate as a dictator over the household. Submission isn't forced—it's voluntary. If you demand submission from an individual, the best you'll get is tolerance.

Christ never demanded submission from the Church. The Church has always been allowed to make a voluntary choice whether or not to be submitted to Jesus. Likewise, husbands aren't to force their wives into submission, but rather to lead them in such way that submission becomes a choice they gladly make.

If husbands and wives simply followed the instructions in Ephesians 5:21–33, the husband would not ask his wife to do things that are unrealistic and irrational. And the wife wouldn't try to take the place of her husband as leader in the home.

If a husband gives himself for his wife and loves her the way Christ loves the Church, she's going to *want* to follow him!

How a Husband Should Love His Wife

What do I mean when I say that your wife will want to follow you if you are loving her the way Christ loves the Church? How does Christ love the Church? When we discover how He loves the Church, we discover how a husband should love his wife. And the Bible clearly gives us the answer in Ephesians chapter 5.

EPHESIANS 5:25–28

25 Husbands, love your wives, just as Christ loved the church and gave himself up for her

26 to make her holy, cleansing her by the washing with water through the word,

27 and to present her to himself as a radiant church, without stain or wrinkle or any other blemish, but holy and blameless.

28 In this same way, husbands ought to love their wives as their own bodies. He who loves his wife loves himself.

If you love your wife as your own body and as Christ loves the Church, you will be more concerned about meeting her needs than you will be about meeting your own! That's what Christ has done for the Church.

Jesus was more interested in meeting our needs than in meeting His own. He gave His life for us! And if we husbands do for our wife what Christ has done for the Church, then all our wife's needs will be met.

If someone in the marriage has to go without new shoes, or new clothes, it should be the husband, not the wife or the children. The Word says Jesus is presenting a *radiant* Church. Our wife should be radiant and well-provided for.

It's easy to submit to someone who cares so much for you that he is willing to sacrifice himself so that you can be blessed. A husband who begins to love his wife as Christ loves the Church will be surprised to see how his wife treats him in return.

The marriage relationship is a two-way street. We need to realize that if husbands, as the head of the house, would "step up to the plate" and do what they're supposed to do in the marriage relationship, their wives would be more willing to do what God designed them to do.

Respecting the Role of Your Mate

Marriage is designed to help two people do together what each person cannot do alone. It is designed to bring increase into their lives.

Someone once said, "Behind every successful man stands a good wife, and a surprised mother-in-law." I don't know about you, but I know that without my wife, I wouldn't be where I am today. I have been blessed because my wife and I have established a relationship based on communication and mutual respect for the other's position in the home.

In more than thirty-five years of marriage, neither of us has ever made a major purchase without discussing it with the other. We have never contradicted each other when disciplining the children. If my wife or I thought the other was wrong, we waited until we were in the privacy of our own bedroom where the children couldn't hear us say, "I think you made a mistake."

I'm talking about a husband and wife having mutual respect for each other's role in the marriage relationship. But really, at the heart of every element of a successful marriage is communication. It's vital to every marriage relationship that spouses develop a communication system whereby they can sit down with each another and talk about everything there is to talk about without either of them getting upset at the other. Effective communication means you sit there and work out problems together.

Sadly, there are many homes today in which the husband and wife cannot sit down and say four or five sentences to each other without being at each other's throats.

A healthy marriage relationship is one in which you both are able to be truthful with each other without becoming offended. In certain situations, you are able to look at yourself and say, "My spouse is right, and I'm wrong." When you get to the place where you can receive what your spouse has to say and then honestly look at yourself and admit you need to change, you're on the way to having a great relationship.

Some men think they are too "macho" to admit they are wrong or need to change. A man who walks all over his wife is not macho—he's weak!

The more you begin to develop your marriage relationship, the closer and more intimate you and your spouse will become. You will reap the rewards and the increase of "two becoming one"— the rewards of treating each other the way God ordained. And your marriage relationship will be more fulfilling than you could ever imagine.

A Strong Marriage Is the Foundation for Success

As we've seen, our lives are made up of different kinds of relationships. We have relationships with one another in our church. We have relationships with neighbors. We have relationships with relatives. We have relationships in many different areas of life. But the marriage relationship is the greatest and the most important relationship you have next to your relationship with your Heavenly Father.

Certainly, our relationship with God must be strong for our marriage relationship to be strong. And when we put God first and develop a strong marriage relationship, we will see a change in our children. Then, once our families are strong, we will see a change in our community, our state, and even in our nation!

Because the marriage relationship is the foundation for our family and our communities, and because it is the greatest of all relationships next to our relationship with God, it is certainly worth the time and effort it takes to make it strong.

Heaven on Earth

I've only scratched the surface in talking about the marriage relationship. I believe the marriage relationship is worth every bit of effort, time, and money it requires to keep it strong. Through marriage, we are able to share our life with someone and become partners together. The marriage relationship helps us understand the kind of relationship God desires to have with us. God wants to share our life. He wants to be our partner.

Remember, man was created first, and God said that it wasn't good for him to be alone. Then God made him a helper. Notice that his helper was not made from a part of his head to dominate and rule over him. Notice also that she wasn't made from the bottom of his feet for him to trample on her. No, woman was taken from man's side, to stand alongside him as his helper. She was taken from his rib—the part of the body near his heart. Therefore, she is to be loved and cared for by her husband.

We can learn from the mistakes Adam and Eve made concerning communication in the marriage relationship. And we can follow the very specific instructions that God gave us in the Bible concerning the marriage relationship.

Ephesians 5:21–28 gives us a godly example of the way a marriage is supposed to function. The man is to be the leader, but the wife is to be right alongside him as they lead their family together. As they work together in unity and harmony with God, their marriage will be the "heaven on earth" it is supposed to be.

Change for the Better

Do you want to change your marriage? Then put God's Word concerning the marriage relationship into practice.

Someone might say, "But that might mean I'm going to have to give up going fishing every Saturday and spend some time with my wife."

If you communicated with her, you might discover that she wants to go fishing with you! And then, you could enjoy things together. There is nothing wrong with a guy going fishing or playing golf. The problem arises when he forgets about his wife and family and spends all his time playing. Problems come when he's never home communicating and spending time with his wife.

As you practice what you've learned, you can establish new communication skills or strengthen the skills you already have and improve your marriage relationship. Every good marriage can be made better. And every difficult marriage can be made a blessed marriage. As we work together in unity and harmony, we can drive strife and division out from our midst. We can have a marriage relationship that's in line with God's Word—one on which God can put His stamp of approval.

One of the reasons you may not be seeing answers to your prayers is that you're not doing what God has already written in His Word. God can't do what He wants to do in your life when you aren't living in line with the Bible.

Come in line with what God's Word has to say, and you will find that your prayers about your marriage will start being answered. If you live in line with God's ways and His Word, things can change for the better!

---

[1]Taken from *A Humorous Look at Love & Marriage* by Bob Phillips. Copyright © 1981 by Harvest House Publishers, Eugene, OR 97402. Used by permission of the author.

CHAPTER SIX

Naomi and Ruth: The Value of Relatives

We've studied the importance of a relationship with God and examined the elements of healthy relationships. Then we looked at the marriage relationship as the most fundamental relationship that exists between two people. Now let's take a closer look at our relationship with our families.

The words "relationship" and "relative" are similar. Both refer to a connection or a kinship.

No matter who we are or what we've experienced, we probably can remember a time when a relative reached out to us with a helping hand or an encouraging word. Maybe a relative gave us an unexpected gift or needed support and assistance. Maybe it was just the reassurance that the relative believed in us. Many of us have treasured memories about our relatives.

I remember the first time I took my wife to a Hagin family get-together. In the Hagin family, there were ten cousins born in a twenty-year span; add to that number all the aunts and uncles, moms and dads, and grandparents. Lynette was quite taken aback

71

at that get-together, because it seemed as if everyone in my family all talked at once. That was some kind of noise!

Since that time, many of my family members have gone on to be with the Lord, but I still have many happy memories of my family.

Family ties are strong. Often, family members will join in other family members' struggles or arguments without even knowing or caring what the fight is about. Some relatives fight each other's battles no matter what.

Have you ever heard of the Hatfields and McCoys from the hills of Kentucky? What began as a dispute between members of the two families turned into a feud that lasted for about thirty years! The Hatfields and McCoys were taught to fight each other years after the original argument—just because their name was either Hatfield or McCoy. By that time, they didn't even know how the feud started! Those are some strong family ties!

Ruth and Naomi

We see how strong family ties were in the biblical story of Ruth and Naomi. We read how the widow Naomi and her daughter-in-law Ruth stayed together after the death of their husbands and returned to Naomi's home of Bethlehem. We see how God then blessed them through one of Naomi's relatives, Boaz.

Let's take a closer look at the story. Naomi was married to a man named Elimelech and they had two sons, Mahlon and Kilion. Because there was a famine in the land of Israel, the family moved to Moab. Soon after, Elimelech died, leaving Naomi alone with her sons. The sons then married Moabite women, Ruth and

Orpah. Then years later, both Mahlon and Kilion died and the three women were left alone in Moab to fend for themselves. When Naomi decided to return to her hometown of Bethlehem, Orpah returned to her parents' home, but Ruth was determined to go to Bethlehem with Naomi.

RUTH 1:15-19

15 "Look," said Naomi, "your sister-in-law is going back to her people and her gods. Go back with her."

16 But Ruth replied, "Don't urge me to leave you or to turn back from you. Where you go I will go, and where you stay I will stay. Your people will be my people and your God my God.

17 Where you die I will die, and there I will be buried. May the Lord deal with me, be it ever so severely, if anything but death separates you and me."

18 When Naomi realized that Ruth was determined to go with her, she stopped urging her.

19 So the two women went on until they came to Bethlehem.

Reading further in the story, we know that Naomi did not have a good outlook on the future. In the society in which she lived, it was the son's responsibility to take care of the family members. In Naomi's case, she had no sons to take care of her. Without her husband and sons, she was destitute. There was no Social Security system, Medicare system, or welfare system to provide for her. Her only hope was Ruth, her daughter-in-law, who had insisted on staying with her for the rest of her life.

The Power of Partnership

Naomi and Ruth had a strong, harmonious, and agreeable relationship. They developed an unshakable relationship, and their kinship provided several things for them. They became partners in life. They had companionship, and they had the privilege of sharing material provision with each other.

RUTH 2:2, 23

2 And Ruth the Moabitess said to Naomi, "Let me go to the fields and pick up the leftover grain behind anyone in whose eyes I find favor." Naomi said to her, "Go ahead, my daughter."

23 So Ruth stayed close to the servant girls of Boaz to glean until the barley and wheat harvests were finished. And she lived with her mother-in-law.

Notice that Naomi and Ruth pooled their resources. Whatever Ruth gleaned in the fields, she shared with her mother-in-law. They shared their lives together, and whatever one had, the other had.

We must learn to share with our relatives. Maybe we're blessed a little more than they are. It won't hurt us to share with them. We are blessed to be a blessing!

Naomi and Ruth also established an agreement in their relationship. Living in agreement allowed God to move in their lives and bless them.

MATTHEW 18:19-20

19 "Again, I tell you that if two of you on earth agree about anything you ask for, it will be done for you by my Father in heaven.

20 For where two or three come together in my name, there am I with them."

Because God dwells in the midst of those who live in unity, we need to learn to live in unity with our relatives. Because unity is important, you can still have a peaceful relationship with your relatives, even if you don't always agree with them.

Ruth flowed in agreement with her mother-in-law. As a result they had a place to live, and they had each other to live with and enjoy companionship.

As I already stated, God made us all to desire companionship with others. If we're married, we enjoy companionship with our spouse. We can also enjoy companionship with our family and our relatives.

You Can Disagree and Still Be Agreeable

Unity is vital to the success of any relationship. We can agree to disagree with our relatives without being disagreeable. We can even agree to disagree with a Christian brother or a sister without being disagreeable with one another.

Unfortunately, some people don't understand this principle. If they happen to disagree with one of their relatives, they have a falling out, or a breach in the relationship. In some families, that breach is never repaired.

Even if you're born again, Spirit-filled, and have a wonderful relationship with God, it is important to maintain a good relationship with your relatives. You need to be ready when God opens the door for you to minister to them, and that is not possible if you don't maintain a relationship with them.

At other times, you may need help from your relatives. It will be easier to ask for and obtain assistance from them if you have maintained a peaceable relationship with them.

Perhaps some of your relatives don't have anyone except you to contact them and show kindness to them. It's important for you to maintain a relationship with them.

It's not necessary to get into strife with relatives. If we learn to walk in love and flow in the kind of relationship Naomi and Ruth had, we can agree to disagree without ever being disagreeable.

Finding Favor Through Relationships

Ruth was blessed through her relationship with Naomi in the sense that she had a partner and friend in life. And because of her relationship with Naomi, Ruth also found favor with Boaz, her kinsman redeemer.

RUTH 2:8-11

8 So Boaz said to Ruth, "My daughter, listen to me. Don't go and glean in another field and don't go away from here. Stay here with my servant girls.

9 Watch the field where the men are harvesting, and follow along after the girls. I have told the men not to touch you. And whenever you are thirsty, go and get a drink from the water jars the men have filled."

10 At this, she bowed down with her face to the ground. She exclaimed, "Why have I found such favor in your eyes that you notice me—a foreigner?"

11 Boaz replied, "I've been told all about what you have done for your mother-in-law since the death of your husband—how you left your father and mother and your homeland and came to live with a people you did not know before."

It was the custom in those days for workers to leave behind whatever wheat they happened to drop in the fields as they were harvesting. In other words, if they dropped any wheat, they didn't pick it up. Then those who were destitute could come along after them and gather the dropped wheat and use it for food or take it to the market and sell it for profit.

Not only did Boaz create a cocoon of protection for Ruth in the fields, but he also instructed his workers to drop wheat on purpose so Ruth could pick it up.

RUTH 2:15-16

15 As she got up to glean, Boaz gave orders to his men, "Even if she gathers among the sheaves, don't embarrass her.

16 Rather, pull out some stalks for her from the bundles and leave them for her to pick up, and don't rebuke her."

Because of the relationship Ruth had established with Naomi and because of the honor she showed Naomi, Ruth obtained favor with Boaz. As a result, Ruth and Naomi received an abundance of food from the field. And Ruth eventually received Boaz as her husband. Ruth received all these blessings simply because she had an agreeable relationship with her mother-in-law.

Ruth's relationship with her relative Naomi put her in a position to become Boaz's wife. It was custom in that day for the nearest relative to marry the widowed woman and care for her. Because of Ruth's loving relationship with Naomi, Boaz, as Ruth's kinsman redeemer, married her and cared for her and her beloved mother-in-law.

When Orpah, Naomi's other daughter-in-law, chose to return to her own people, Ruth chose to stay with Naomi. And she not only received the blessings of a close relationship with her mother-in-law, but she also received a new husband through being so closely united with her relative.

You may not agree with everything your relatives do and say, but you can find things upon which you do agree upon. Having an agreeable relationship with relatives will put you in a position of increase. You will be blessed, and you will also be able to be a blessing to your family.

Good Relative, Good Witness

Because Ruth maintained a relationship with Naomi, she became a matriarch from whose family line Jesus descended. You see, maintaining strong relationships with your relatives may mean a blessing for someone somewhere down the road, so to speak.

Many people have written off or disowned their relatives because the relatives did something they didn't like. But if you write your relatives off and have nothing to do with them, how can you expect to present Christ to them? There may be a time when you are the only one who can share Christ with your relatives. But if you don't have a relationship with them, they won't be willing to listen to what you have to say.

And, as I said, there may be times when your relatives are the only people left to whom *you* can turn in a time of need. If you don't have a relationship with them already, how can you go to them for help when you need it most?

Restoration in Relationships

Do you have relationships with relatives that you would like to see restored? God wants to bless the relationships you have with your relatives. Start believing for this to happen in your life. You can use your faith for many different things, because the Bible says the just shall live by faith (Rom. 1:17). So begin to confess and believe for a restored relationship with a relative who may be estranged from the family. Confess it by faith just as you use your faith for healing or finances. God will move on that situation and begin to restore that relationship.

Just as you may have had to stand in faith for a length of time as you believed God for your finances, or some other blessing, you may have to stand in faith for a period of time for the restoration of family relationships.

If the devil tries to tell you that it's never going to happen, boldly confess, "In the Name of Jesus, I believe what the Word says. The Word says that if I believe in my heart and confess with my mouth, I shall have what I say [Rom. 10:10, Mark 11:23]. I'm confessing a healthy relationship with my relatives! And I thank God for it now!"

I've told people to do this, and I've seen it work. If God did it for anyone else, He'll do it for you.

Relationships Bring Blessing

The most important lesson to be learned from the story of Naomi, Ruth, and Boaz is that the blessings of God often come through relationships. Ruth and Naomi were blessed because of the relationship they established and maintained with each other. Relationships with your relatives are very important!

I'm sure there are times when you haven't wanted to claim some of your relatives as your own. We have all been there! But they're still your relatives. And if you cut them out of your life, you may never have an opportunity to help them change. If everyone else in your family cuts them off, your maintaining a godly relationship with them could be the one thing that may help turn their life around.

Pray for Your Family

Spend time praying for your relatives. Pray for those who need to be saved. Pray that God will send laborers across their path—people whom they respect and to whom they will listen. Pray for the safety and well-being of your relatives. Pray for an opportunity to show God's love to them in some tangible way. But when you do, be ready to do something for them. You may have to reach into your billfold and give them some money. Showing God's love doesn't mean lecturing them or giving them a sermon. I'm talking about doing something in a tangible way to show them how much God loves them!

Maybe you need to pray for a relative who has wronged or abused you. Now is the time to forgive them. After you have prayed for them and forgiven them, don't think about the past any more. Don't allow the old hurt to come in. As you forgive them, the Holy Spirit will apply His healing balm to heal the wound, so don't open it back up by thinking about it.

Someone asked, "Just how do I pray for my family members?" Pray that God will use you to minister to them in some way to be a blessing to them. And, finally, pray that God will help you build and maintain a strong relationship with all your relatives. Remember, there's blessing in relationships!

CHAPTER SEVEN

A Covenant Relationship With God

In our study of relationships, we've seen that the first and foremost relationship we must establish is our relationship with God. We've also examined the elements of healthy friendship relationships, the marriage relationship, and family relationships.

Remember, *relationship* is defined as "connection, kinship, or involvement." In this chapter, I want to study a different kind of relationship—the covenant relationship a man can have with God. Abraham serves as an excellent example of a man who had a covenant relationship with God.

Abraham is probably one of the most well-known and most talked about people in the Bible. Many people are mentioned in the Old Testament, and many are mentioned in the New Testament. But Abraham is mentioned throughout the entire Word of God.

Through Abraham, there exists not only a nation of natural descendants, but also a nation of spiritual descendants. As Christians, we are the spiritual children of Abraham (Gal. 3:29)!

Abraham's relationship with God influenced generation upon generation after him. He had a tremendous relationship with God. Abraham has been called "The Father of Israel," "The Father of Faith," and "The Friend of God."

The Attitudes of Abraham's Heart

Let's look at Abraham's life and discover some of the attitudes of his heart—attitudes that enabled him to have a covenant relationship with God.

Number one, *Abraham obeyed God implicitly.* When God told him to leave his family and go to another country, he obeyed immediately. Even though he didn't know where he was going, he knew he was going *somewhere* because he was obeying God!

At one point in his journey, people asked him where he was going. He said that he was "looking for a city," a place where once he arrived, God would tell him he was where He wanted him to be (see Genesis 12)!

Most Christians want God to show them the whole picture before they ever start obeying Him. That's the reason some people never go anywhere spiritually. You have to start out in simple faith and obedience, and when you get there, God will let you know!

GENESIS 12:4–8

4 So Abram [Notice his name is still Abram at this point. He didn't become "Abraham" until he had a covenant with God] **left, as the Lord had told him; and Lot went with him. Abram was seventy-five years old when he set out from Haran.**

5 He took his wife Sarai [not Sarah yet], **his nephew Lot, all the possessions they had accumulated and the people they had acquired in Haran, and they set out for the land of Canaan, and they arrived there.**

6 Abram traveled through the land as far as the site of the great tree of Moreh at Shechem. At that time the Canaanites were in the land.

7 The Lord appeared to Abram and said, "To your offspring I will give this land." So he built an altar there to the Lord, who had appeared to him.

8 From there he went on towards the hills east of Bethel and pitched his tent, with Bethel on the west and Ai on the east. There he built an altar to the Lord and called on the name of the Lord.

Abraham was chosen to have a covenant relationship with God because, number one, he followed and obeyed God implicitly. Number two, *Abraham worshipped God.* Wherever he traveled, he built an altar to worship God.

We just read Genesis 12:8, which says, *"From there he went on towards the hills east of Bethel and pitched his tent, with Bethel on the west and Ai on the east. There he built an altar to the Lord and called on the name of the Lord."* We see it again in Genesis 13:4, Genesis 13:18, and Genesis 21:33. The last verse does not say that he built an altar, but it says that he prayed and worshipped God.

Not only did Abraham obey God and worship God, but number three, *he believed God.*

GENESIS 15:6

6 Abram BELIEVED THE LORD, and he credited it to him as righteousness.

The Bible says that when God promised Abraham a child, he did not stagger at the promise of God. In other words, when God said it, Abraham believed it!

Let's see what the New Testament has to say about Abraham.

ROMANS 4:19-22

19 Without weakening in his faith, he [Abraham] faced the fact that his body was as good as dead—since he was about a hundred years old—and that Sarah's womb was also dead.

20 Yet he did not waver through unbelief regarding the promise of God, but was strengthened in his faith and gave glory to God,

21 being fully persuaded that God had power to do what he had promised.

22 This is why "it was credited to him as righteousness."

Here we find a correlation between what the Old Testament says about Abraham believing God and what Paul says about him in the New Testament. The Bible says that Abraham believed God!

As Christians, it is our belief in the Lord Jesus Christ that is credited to us as righteousness. In other words, we become righteous by believing in the Lord Jesus Christ. Abraham also believed God, and it was credited unto him as righteousness.

A Relationship Takes Two!

God and Abraham chose to have a relationship with one another. God chose to have a relationship with Abraham, and Abraham responded to God by choosing a relationship with Him. For any relationship to work, whether it's a spiritual relationship between God and man or a natural relationship between two people, it has to be by mutual choice.

Every kind of relationship takes two! You can't have a relationship with someone if he or she is not reciprocating. It doesn't matter how badly you want it. Unless the other person reciprocates, there's no relationship. You may think there is, but there's not! A true relationship cannot be developed unless there is a connection between two.

God spoke to Abraham and told him the covenant would be with him and his seed. It's because of this covenant promise God made to Abraham and his seed that we, too, have the covenant because according to the New Testament, we are the spiritual children of Abraham.

GALATIANS 3:7

7 **Understand, then, that those who believe are children of Abraham.**

Because we believe in the Lord Jesus Christ, we are considered Abraham's seed and partakers in the covenant!

Terms of the Covenant

When God established the covenant with Abraham, He told him what the covenant provisions would be and what Abraham had to do to comply with the covenant and receive the blessing.

GENESIS 17:1-8

1 **When Abram was ninety-nine years old, the Lord appeared to him and said, "I am God Almighty; walk before me and be blameless.**

2 **I will confirm my covenant between me and you and will greatly increase your numbers."**

3 **Abram fell facedown, and God said to him,**

4 **"As for me, this is my covenant with you: You will be the father of many nations.**

5 **No longer will you be called Abram; your name will be Abraham, for I have made you a father of many nations** [the name "Abraham" means father of many nations].

6 **I will make you very fruitful; I will make nations of you, and kings will come from you.**

7 **I will establish my covenant as an everlasting covenant between me and you and your descendants after you for the generations to come, to be your God and the God of your descendants after you.**

8 The whole land of Canaan, where you are now an alien, I will give as an everlasting possession to you and your descendants after you; and I will be their God."

God told Abraham that He would keep a covenant with him and what His part in the covenant would be. As we read further, we see that God also said that *Abraham* had a part to fulfill in the covenant.

Abraham had a choice whether or not to accept the terms of the covenant. You also have a choice. You can choose to have a covenant relationship with God and enjoy all the benefits named in the Word of God. Or you can choose to go your own way, live the way you want to live in a devil's world, and go to a devil's hell.

Now I know that it is not popular or "politically correct" to mention the word "hell," but hell is a reality. And without a relationship with God through His Son Jesus Christ, you will spend eternity in hell. I'm just telling you what the Bible says. But if you choose to have a relationship with God by accepting Jesus as your Savior and believing upon the blood that He shed on Calvary, you will spend eternity in Heaven.

It is your choice to make, not God's!

Someone might say, "Why would God send people to hell?"

God doesn't send people to hell! People make their *own* choice about where they will spend eternity.

When a criminal is sentenced in court, the judge isn't the one responsible for the fact that the criminal is sentenced to prison. He sentenced himself when he broke the law. The judge simply pronounces what the law says regarding a given situation.

In the same way, a person sentences himself to hell when he fails to accept Jesus as Savior. God has given you a choice. Deuteronomy 30:19 says, *"I call heaven and earth to record this day against you, that I have set before you life and death, blessing and cursing: therefore CHOOSE LIFE . . ."* (KJV).

The Bible is God talking to all mankind. And in it God said, "I'm going to give you a choice. I'm going to send My Son. He's going to die for you. And if you choose to believe on Him, you will be justified. If you choose *not* to believe on Him, you will be condemned." That's just the way it is!

It's important to understand that when you let an opportunity to accept Jesus Christ as Savior pass you by, you are making a choice, either consciously or unconsciously, to reject Jesus as your Savior. In effect, you are also choosing against God!

Abraham had a choice to make. He chose to accept the terms of the covenant with God. What were the covenant terms? Let's read Genesis 17:9–11.

GENESIS 17:9–11

9 Then God said to Abraham, "As for you, you must keep my covenant, you and your descendants after you for the generations to come.

10 This is my covenant with you and your descendants after you, the covenant you are to keep: Every male among you shall be circumcised.

11 You are to undergo circumcision, and it will be the sign of the covenant between me and you."

Abraham accepted these terms and lived his life by them. And, of course, God abided by His terms of the covenant, and Abraham was greatly blessed.

Covenant Communication

Throughout his life, Abraham enjoyed a continuing conversation with God. As we've seen in previous chapters, communication is vital in any good relationship. You can't have a good relationship with someone if you can't communicate with one another.

Not only did Abraham talk with God, but God talked and consulted with Abraham.

GENESIS 18:17-22

17 Then the Lord said, "Shall I hide from Abraham what I am about to do?

18 Abraham will surely become a great and powerful nation, and all nations on earth will be blessed through him.

19 For I have chosen him, so that he will direct his children and his household after him to keep the way of the Lord by doing what is right and just, so that the Lord will bring about for Abraham what he has promised him."

20 Then the Lord said, "The outcry against Sodom and Gomorrah is so great and their sin so grievous

21 that I will go down and see if what they have done is as bad as the outcry that has reached me. If not, I will know."

22 The men turned away and went towards Sodom, but Abraham remained standing before the Lord.

In this passage of scripture, the Lord began to talk to Abraham about what was going on in Sodom and Gomorrah. Because of their covenant relationship, God chose not to hide from Abraham what He was going to do. He talked it over with him and gave him a chance to intercede (Gen. 18:23-33).

Did you know that if you have a relationship with God through Jesus Christ, you can talk things over with Him and He will talk to you? It can happen through prayer, and you can also hear from God by reading what He has already said to you in His Word.

People who say, "God never talks to me" must not read their Bible. If you read the Bible, then God talks to you, because the Bible is God talking to you!

Friend of God

God not only talked to Abraham, but He considered him a friend. Genesis 18:19 says, *"For I know him, that he will command his children and his household after him, and they shall keep the way of the Lord, to do justice and judgment; that the Lord may bring upon Abraham that which he hath spoken of him"* (KJV). The phrase "I know him" in this verse means God knew Abraham as an acquaintance, familiar friend, and kinsman.

God referred to Abraham as a familiar friend. What kind of relationship do you have with God? Do you consider God a friend of yours? Does God consider you a friend of His? God referred to Abraham as a kinsman. Are you God's son or daughter? Can He say, "I know you"? These are important questions for you to ponder.

In Genesis 18:20, God and Abraham begin sharing their hearts with one another. God tells Abraham that He's going to destroy Sodom and Gomorrah, and Abraham begins to bargain with God to try to save those wicked cities for the sake of his nephew and Lot's family.

GENESIS 18:23-33

23 THEN ABRAHAM APPROACHED HIM [God] AND SAID: "Will you sweep away the righteous with the wicked?

24 What if there are fifty righteous people in the city? Will you really sweep it away and not spare the place for the sake of the fifty righteous people in it?

25 Far be it from you to do such a thing—to kill the righteous with the wicked, treating the righteous and the wicked alike. Far be it from you! Will not the Judge of all the earth do right?"

26 The Lord said, "If I find fifty righteous people in the city of Sodom, I will spare the whole place for their sake."

27 THEN ABRAHAM SPOKE UP AGAIN: "Now that I have been so bold as to speak to the Lord, though I am nothing but dust and ashes,

28 what if the number of the righteous is five less than fifty? Will you destroy the whole city because of five people?" "If I find forty-five there," he said, "I will not destroy it."

29 ONCE AGAIN HE SPOKE TO HIM, "What if only forty are found there?" He said, "For the sake of forty, I will not do it."

30 THEN HE SAID, "May the Lord not be angry, but let me speak. What if only thirty can be found there?" He answered, "I will not do it if I find thirty there."

31 ABRAHAM SAID, "Now that I have been so bold as to speak to the Lord, what if only twenty can be found there?" He said, "For the sake of twenty, I will not destroy it."

32 THEN HE [Abraham] SAID, "May the Lord not be angry, but let me speak just once more. What if only ten can be found there?" He answered, "For the sake of ten, I will not destroy it."

33 When the Lord had finished speaking with Abraham, he left, and Abraham returned home.

In this passage, we see Abraham bargaining with the Lord. When the Lord tells him that He is going to destroy the city, Abraham says, "Well, now, wait a minute. There might be some righteous people living there. If there are fifty righteous people, will You spare the city?"

The Lord said, "Okay, if there are fifty righteous in the city, I will spare it."

Abraham got a little bolder, and he kept lowering the number of righteous until the Lord agreed to spare the city if just ten righteous people could be found there.

Evidently, they couldn't find ten righteous people, because the city was destroyed. Lot, his wife, and his two daughters must have been the only righteous people, because they were the only ones who were spared.

Notice that Abraham and God talked with one another. They shared their hearts with each other. God shared His plan, and Abraham shared his concern. As God shares plans with you, are you able to share your concerns with Him? If you have a proper relationship with Him, you can!

Sharing your heart with one another is a vital key to relationships. In your relationship with God, your spouse, and your relatives—*in every relationship*—being able to share your heart with one another is a vital key! There is no genuine relationship unless you can communicate heart-to-heart.

Sharing Heart to Heart

When I was growing up, I remember the houses with the big front porches where people would gather and have heart-to-heart conversations in the evenings. When I was a child, there was a neighbor farmer who would walk down to our house and talk to my grandpa. In the cool of the evening, they would sit out on the big porch in rocking chairs. They shared heart-to-heart with one another about their farms, crops, animals, and so forth.

They had a relationship with one another and with their other neighbors. And if something happened to a neighbor's farm, everyone in the area showed up to help him put his barn back up or harvest his crops.

With our big cities today, I think we have lost a special kind of relationship with fellow members of our community. In most cities, homes are not built with big porches. Therefore, neighbors don't sit and talk like they used to. In fact, most people don't even know their neighbors' names.

Everyone is so busy these days; two neighbors might wave at each other as they both leave to go to work in the morning. They might recognize each other on the street, but they have no relationship whatsoever. As I said, you have to take the time to share your heart and learn what's going on in another person's life to have a relationship with him.

Sharing Your Concerns With God

Notice that in Genesis chapter 18, God was willing to adjust His plans because Abraham was concerned about the people in Sodom. Abraham's relatives lived there, so he was concerned about them. And God was willing to adjust His plans just for Abraham's sake.

Do you understand that if you have a relationship with God, you can share your concerns with Him? And when He shares His plans with you—if you are in a covenant relationship with Him as Abraham was—He will work with you concerning your desires in the situation.

If God would work with Abraham and alter His plan for him, then why wouldn't God work with you, a spiritual descendent of Abraham? God said He was going to have a covenant with us through Abraham, so why couldn't we share our heart with Him today the way Abraham did and find that perhaps He will alter His plans for our sake?

Now I realize this idea is going to step on some theological toes, so to speak. Some people might say, "Well, I don't agree with that, because God is sovereign." I understand that God is sovereign. But we have a biblical example of God's willingness to alter His plan after His covenant son shared his thoughts and concerns with Him about the plan.

I believe that if God speaks to us about things concerning us or our family, we can say, "Lord, I have some concerns about such-and-such. Are there some adjustments we can make?" I believe that God would allow some adjustments to be made. I think so because I have a biblical example in Abraham—our father in the faith!

Abraham discussed things with God, and they arrived at a mutual agreement. Discussing issues and being willing to make adjustments is another vital key in relationships.

Follow Abraham's Example

Abraham had such a close relationship with God that he was called "God's friend."

JAMES 2:23

23 And the scripture was fulfilled that says, "Abraham believed God, and it was credited to him as righteousness," and he was called God's friend.

If you're born again and have a covenant relationship with God, you, too, are God's friend. But the question I ask you today is, "Are you taking advantage of the covenant you have with God?" Are you communicating with God on a regular basis? Are you reading His Word and spending time in prayer? Are you spending time worshipping God? Are you sharing your heart with God? Are you discussing things with God before you do them? And are you willing to follow and obey God implicitly?

Is it possible for you to have the kind of relationship with God that Abraham had? The answer is, emphatically, *yes*. Abraham is an example for us of what we can have with God through believing on the Lord Jesus Christ and living according to God's Word.

Determine in your heart today that you are going to walk according to God's Word. Make the decision today to live in a covenant relationship with God the way Abraham did. When you walk in God's ways and live in covenant with Him, you will receive the blessing of Abraham. And you will be called God's friend!

CHAPTER EIGHT

The Value of Friendship

In our study of relationships, we've seen that the first and foremost relationship we must establish is our relationship with God. We've examined the elements of healthy relationships, the marriage relationship, and the relationship we have with our relatives. We've also studied the covenant relationship that Abraham had with God.

As we continue our study on relationships, let's see what the Bible has to say about the value of friendship.

JOHN 15:12-17

12 My command is this: Love each other as I have loved you.

13 Greater love has no one than this, that he lay down his life for his friends.

14 You are my friends if you do what I command.

15 I no longer call you servants, because a servant does not know his master's business. Instead, I have called you friends, for everything that I learned from my Father I have made known to you.

16 You did not choose me, but I chose you and appointed you to go and bear fruit—fruit that will last. Then the Father will give you whatever you ask in my name.

17 This is my command: Love each other.

In this passage, Jesus Himself says He is our friend. There is an old hymn that says, "What a friend we have in Jesus, all our sins and griefs to bear! What a privilege to carry everything to God in prayer!"[1] As Christians, Jesus is our friend. But we must also realize our need for friendship with other people.

It is a fact of life that you must have friends if you are going to accomplish very much. People need someone to believe in them in order for them to accomplish anything worthwhile.

Jesse Owens, one of the greatest athletes this country has ever known, witnessed the value of friendship at the 1936 Olympic games. That year, the summer Olympics were held in Berlin, Germany, and Adolf Hitler was in power. Hitler wanted to prove that his athletes were the best in the world.

Owens had set a world record the previous year in the running broad jump, but on the day of the Olympic competition, he missed his first two qualifying jumps. Then a German jumper, the toughest competitor Owens faced in that event, suggested he start his qualifying jump a few inches behind the take-off board. Owens did that, qualified, and went on to win the gold medal and set an Olympic record that stood for more than twenty years. And the German jumper who had helped him was the first to congratulate him!

What that German athlete did for Jesse Owens was a demonstration of true friendship. And that gesture was something Owens remembered the rest of his life.

Destined to Be Friends With Jesus

I want to share three facts about friendship with you. Fact number one, *you were destined to have Jesus as your best friend.*

The Word of God tells us that it was ordained before the foundation of the world. Friendship with Jesus is the will of God concerning you! Jesus wants to be your friend and help you through life. He has forgiven you of your sins. He wants to show you how to overcome and "win the gold" in the game of life.

Notice the characteristics of friendship that Jesus shared in John 15:12–17. First, a *friend* is someone who *loves* you. John 15:12 says, *"My command is this: Love each other as I have loved you."* We know that Jesus is a true friend because He loves us.

Second, a *friend* is someone who *gives his life for you.* John 15:13 says, *"Greater love has no one than this, that he lay down his life for his friends."* Jesus showed His great love for us in that while we were still sinners, He died for us (Rom. 5:8).

Third, a *friend* is someone who *does something for you when you ask him to do it.* A true friend won't make excuses when asked to do something; a friend will just do it! John 15:14 says, *"You are my friends if you do what I command."*

Fourth, a *friend* is someone who *shares himself with you.* In John 15:15, Jesus said, *"I no longer call you servants, because a servant does not know his master's business. Instead, I have called you friends, for everything that I learned from my Father I have made known to you."* Jesus shared His heart with His disciples, and He still shares His heart with us today.

Fifth, a *friend* is someone who *chooses you voluntarily.* John 15:16 says, *"You did not choose me, but I chose you and appointed you to go and bear fruit—fruit that will last. Then the Father will give you whatever you ask in my name."* Notice that we didn't choose Jesus—*He chose us!* And in order for you to enter a friendship relationship with Jesus and enjoy the benefits of friendship with Him, you must choose Him voluntarily too. Jesus won't force His friendship on you.

Sixth, a *friend* is someone who *still believes in you* when everyone else gives up on you. In John 15:17, Jesus said, *"This is my command: Love each other."* Jesus would not command you to do something that He was unwilling to do. He will always love you. Even if the whole world gives up on you, Jesus still believes in you! He is your friend!

Created With a Need for Friends

From the passage in John chapter 15, you see fact number one: *You were destined to have Jesus as your best friend.* This is fact number two: *You were created with a need for friends.*

Look at Adam, for example. Though he was a perfect creation, had daily fellowship with God, and lived in a perfect environment, God said, "It is not good for man to be alone" (Gen. 2:18).

Even though you know God and have Jesus as your friend, you still need other people. You can be the most spiritual person on earth and have the most spiritual experiences known to man, but you still need earthly friends.

There are three levels of interaction that fulfill a need in peoples' lives: Level one is *relationship*, which involves a kinship or connection. Level two is *fellowship*, which involves communion, partnership, and sharing. And level three is *friendship*—a mutual attachment marked by devotion, affection, regard, and esteem. (We will study this in greater detail in the next chapter.)

God has divinely appointed the paths of certain people to intersect with your life and enrich you. There are certain people with whom I have had contact over the years who are truly my friends. And even though I may not see them for a very long time, I can call them on the phone and talk as though we've never been apart. They are whom I consider divinely appointed friends!

Friendship also allows a networking to take place so that your efforts will accomplish multiplied times more than what you could do by yourself. Looking back, you could probably say that without a certain friendship, without the encouragement of a certain friend, you would not be where you are today. Friendship is valuable and vital to our success in life.

Ordained to Be a Friend

Friendship fact number one is you were *destined to have Jesus as your best friend.* Fact number two is you *were created with a need for friends.* And this is fact number three: *You were ordained to be a friend to others.*

Not only were you created to *need* a friend, you were also ordained to *be* a friend. Someone is waiting for you! Someone needs your friendship! And you will never be totally fulfilled until you have reached out to others and become their friend.

We've gotten so busy in this modern world that we don't seem to have time to spend with our friends. Everyone is busy doing his own thing, but we won't be fulfilled until we make time to be with friends.

When I was growing up, I almost always went to lunch after church with one of my friends. I thank God for those memories, and I thank God for the friendships I built. I still stay in touch with those friends today, and they are still valuable to me.

Choose Your Friends Wisely

Well, if we were ordained to be friends with people, how should we choose our friends? Most people choose their friends with no criteria at all. Their friends consist of anyone who is friendly to them. But that doesn't work! You need to choose your friends wisely.

It's been said that loyalty is the lifeblood of real friendship. Invest deeply in a few friends rather than superficially among many. Select your friends carefully, and then stick with them.

How can you carefully select friends? Here are a few guidelines to help you choose your friends wisely:

(1) Choose people who have similar interests, beliefs, morals, and values.

(2) Choose friends who will support you, strengthen you, and encourage you to do the will of God.

(3) Choose people who are going the same direction in life that you are.

(4) Choose people who will add something of value to your life.

(5) Choose people who will lift you up, not pull you down.

An author of one book talked about basement people and balcony people. You don't want to choose "basement people" for friends. Now what do I mean when I say "basement people"? Those are people who will pull you down. They will tell you that you can't do it, that you can't make it, and that you might as well quit! Basement people will keep you living at a lower level than the level God destined you to achieve.

Choose your friends among "balcony people"—people who will pull you up to a higher level of life! They will surround you with words of faith and encouragement, saying, "Yes, you can make it! You can do it! You can be all that God destined you to be!"[2]

Your choice of friends many times will determine your way of life. Choose people who will lift you up to a higher level instead of people who will pull you down.

Three Facts of Friendship

In this chapter, I've shown you that *you were destined to have a friend in Jesus.* Jesus should be your best friend.

The second fact of friendship that I've shown you is that *you were created with a need for friends.* And, fact number three, *you were ordained to be a friend to someone else.* Let's review the details from John 15:12–17 of the characteristics of true friendship—the kind of friendship you will find with Jesus.

- A friend is someone who loves you in spite of everything, no matter what.

- A friend is someone who sticks up for you, gives himself for you, and doesn't bail out on you when the going gets rough.

- A friend is someone who does something when you ask him to do it instead of making a lot of excuses for why they can't do it.

- A friend is someone with whom you can share your life.

- A friend is someone you choose voluntarily.

- A friend is someone who when the world gives up on you still says, "Hey, you're all right with me. I still believe in you."

Friends in the Bible

Throughout the Word of God we see godly friendships. Daniel was a friend of Shadrach, Meshach, and Abednego. Elijah and Elisha were friends as well as mentor and student. We'll study in the next chapter the strong friendship between David and Jonathan, and later, we will study Paul's life and learn from the friendships he maintained.

Jesus had twelve disciples, but Peter, James, and John were His closest friends. Remember the Mount of Transfiguration and the Garden of Gethsemane? When it came to sharing intimate things, Jesus singled out Peter, James, and John.

Friends in Need Are Friends Indeed

A true friend will fight for you in your hour of need. A true friend will be there to defend you. It helps in the hour of need to have someone who will stand beside you and say, "I believe in you." When you think you can't go any further, it makes all the difference in the world to have someone pat you on the back and say, "You can make it. I appreciate you and believe in you."

Sometimes all it takes is a pat on the back or a little word of encouragement to push you over the top. That is why godly friendships are so vitally important.

When our son, Craig, was in the eighth grade, he had an operation to remove a brain tumor. It helped to have friends pray for us, love us, and give us strength. I am so glad we had the kind of friends who were willing and able to pray with us and believe God with us.

I never will forget sitting in the waiting room after Craig's surgery. I was waiting while Craig was recuperating in Intensive Care. My wife came over to me and told me that a pastor friend of mine and his wife were in the lobby. I went out to meet them and talk with them.

On my way out to the lobby I thought to myself, *They're probably just passing through Tulsa on their way home to Dallas and are stopping by just for a moment.* As it happened, when this man and his wife heard the news about Craig, they drove up from Dallas just to spend the day with us.

That was an act of true friendship! He sacrificed his Saturday when he could have been preparing for his two Sunday morning services, his Sunday night service, and a live television broadcast that he filmed on Sunday at midnight. I will never forget that act of kindness he showed me. His friendship supported me when I needed it most.

You see, a friend will sacrifice for you. A friend will be there when you need a helping hand. And that is why having friends is so important.

I challenge you to develop godly friendships. Don't wait until tomorrow; start today. The right kind of friends can help you achieve your goals and dreams and reach your potential. Choose your friends wisely, and in being a friend to others, choose to be the kind of friend Jesus is to you.

---

[1]From *"What a Friend We Have in Jesus"* by Joseph Scriven.

[2]Adapted from *Balcony People* by Joyce Landorf Heatherley. Used by permission.

CHAPTER NINE

David and Jonathan: Friends Forever

So far, we've seen that God wants you to have a personal relationship with Him and that He created you to have relationships with other people. We've also studied the elements of a healthy relationship. We then learned about Adam and Eve's example of the marriage relationship. We studied Naomi and Ruth and discovered the value of relatives. We learned about the covenant relationship that Abraham had with God and that *we* can have through Jesus Christ. And in the previous chapter, we studied another aspect of relationships: *friendship.*

In studying what the Bible has to say about friendship, we find a very good example of true friendship in the story of David and Jonathan.

1 SAMUEL 18:1-4

1 After David had finished talking with Saul, Jonathan became one in spirit with David, and he loved him as himself.

2 From that day Saul kept David with him and did not let him return to his father's house.

3 And Jonathan made a covenant with David because he loved him as himself.

4 Jonathan took off the robe he was wearing and gave it to David, along with his tunic [his coat], and even his sword, his bow and his belt.

It's obvious from reading Scripture that David and Jonathan became closer to each other than they were to their own family members. Many people have friends who are closer to them than family members. Proverbs 18:24 says, *"A man of many companions may come to ruin, but there is a friend who sticks closer than a brother."* Jesus Christ is the Christian's friend who stays closer than a brother.

Relationship, Fellowship, Friendship

Friendship is vitally important in our lives. Sometimes our friends make the difference for us between victory and defeat. Many people can say that it's because of a certain friend that they were able to succeed in life.

John C. Maxwell, in his book *The Treasure of a Friend*, said, "Your companions are like the buttons on an elevator. They will either take you up, or they will take you down." And Henry Ford is quoted as saying, "My best friend is the one who brings out the best in me."

I believe that if we want to experience the real treasure in life besides our relationship with Jesus Christ and our relationship with our spouse and children, we need to make some true friends. Friends are such an important part of life—what a treasure we would lose if we forgot to make friends!

Friendships extend a lot deeper than a simple relationship. We must realize that there are three levels of interaction common to most people: *Relationship,* which is a kinship or connection; *fellowship,* which involves communion, partnership, and sharing; and *friendship,* which involves a mutual attachment in which two people are devoted to one another and have mutual affection, regard, and esteem for one another.

Notice the progression of each level of interaction from *relationship,* in which people are simply connected, to *friendship,* in which there is a mutual attachment. Relationships are the basis for fellowship and friendship. Fellowship and friendship cannot occur without relationships first being established.

You can have relationships with many people, but true friendship only occurs with a few people. As you go through your daily life, you can look around and see the different levels of relationships you have with the people you know. Although you may have a relationship, or connection, with lots of people—at work, in the community, in your church—very few of those people might qualify as a true friend, or what we might call a kindred spirit.

And that's not to say anything bad about your relationships with the people with whom you feel connected. I'm not undermining the importance of those relationships or putting them in a second-class category. There is just something special about the deep, lasting friendships you have with a few people.

What Is a Friend?

What exactly is a friend? I like to use the following acrostic to define the word friend.

F—A friend is *faithful* and loyal to the other person on a consistent basis, no matter what others say or do.

R—Friends are *real* and true to each other without hypocrisy or flattery.

I—Friends are *interested* in similar things and in what each other likes to do.

E—Friends *enjoy* being in the company of each other.

N—Friends *never* leave nor forsake the other person in good or bad times.

D—Friends *dare* to believe in the other person even when other people do not and are putting him or her down.

These six elements of friendship are the things that will bind you and another person together. The first element is faithfulness. You're not a true friend if you're only around in fair weather. You're not a true friend if you jump and run at the slightest hint of a problem.

David and Jonathan were true friends. They stood by each other through good times and bad. Even when Jonathan's own father, the king, turned against David, Jonathan stood by him. He and David both understood what a covenant of friendship truly means.

1 SAMUEL 20:16–17

16 So Jonathan made a covenant with the house of David, saying, "May the Lord call David's enemies to account."

17 And Jonathan made David reaffirm his oath out of love for him, because he loved him as he loved himself.

David and Jonathan remained friends in the midst of trouble, opposition, and accusations. The story of David and Jonathan demonstrates the value of having friends who stay through the thick and the thin—friends who stay in spite of circumstances!

King Saul, Jonathan's father, wanted to destroy this friendship between David and Jonathan. And in First Samuel chapter 20 we see why.

1 SAMUEL 20:30-33

30 Saul's anger flared up at Jonathan and he said to him, "You son of a perverse and rebellious woman! Don't I know that you have sided with the son of Jesse to your own shame and to the shame of the mother who bore you?

31 As long as the son of Jesse lives on this earth, neither you nor your kingdom will be established. Now send and bring him to me, for he must die!"

32 "Why should he be put to death? What has he done?" Jonathan asked his father.

33 But Saul hurled his spear at him to kill him. Then Jonathan knew that his father intended to kill David.

Jonathan was in line as heir to Saul's throne. But Samuel the prophet had anointed David to be king after Saul. Saul wanted his son Jonathan to be king, so he tried to kill David to make it possible. But Jonathan understood the workings of God. He defended David to his father and made him so mad that Saul threw a spear at his own son!

The Devil Wants to Destroy Your Relationships!

The devil used Saul to try to destroy the friendship between David and Jonathan. The devil wants to destroy relationships. He delights in separating people. He delights in stopping the potential that exists when strong relationships are built. He delights in bringing strife, division, and unrest between people.

Ever since the devil was kicked out of Heaven, he's been trying to keep people from having a relationship with God. When you have a strong relationship with God, you can have strong relationships with your fellow Christians. There can be no strong relationship, or friendship, with your fellow brother or sister in the Lord unless you first have a strong relationship with the Father.

In the natural, we have a relationship with our siblings because we all identify with our father. In the Body of Christ, we can have a relationship with one another because we identify with our Heavenly Father.

An Inheritance of Favor

Despite Saul's actions, David and Jonathan demonstrated the true characteristics of friendship. Again, Jonathan, son of Saul, was next in the royal line of succession. Notice he didn't get offended that David had been anointed as king instead. Jonathan remained a true friend all of his life; he and David had a covenant relationship together.

Because of the faithfulness of Jonathan's friendship with David, Jonathan's son Mephibosheth inherited the blessings and favor of King David and enjoyed those blessings long after Jonathan's death.

2 SAMUEL 9:1-10

1 David asked, "Is there anyone still left of the house of Saul to whom I can show kindness FOR JONATHAN'S SAKE?"

2 Now there was a servant of Saul's household named Ziba. They called him to appear before David, and the king said to him, "Are you Ziba?" "Your servant," he replied.

3 The king asked, "Is there no one still left of the house of Saul to whom I can show God's kindness?" Ziba answered the king, "There is still a son of Jonathan; he is crippled in both feet."

4 "Where is he?" the king asked. Ziba answered, "He is at the house of Makir son of Ammiel in Lo Debar."

5 So King David had him brought from Lo Debar, from the house of Makir son of Ammiel.

6 When Mephibosheth son of Jonathan, the son of Saul, came to David, he bowed down to pay him honor. David said, "Mephibosheth!" "Your servant," he replied.

7 "Don't be afraid," David said to him, "for I will surely show you kindness for the sake of your father Jonathan. I will restore to you all the land that belonged to your grandfather Saul, and you will always eat at my table."

8 Mephibosheth bowed down and said, "What is your servant, that you should notice a dead dog like me?"

9 Then the king summoned Ziba, Saul's servant, and said to him, "I have given your master's grandson everything that belonged to Saul and his family.

10 You and your sons and your servants are to farm the land for him and bring in the crops, so that your master's grandson may be provided for. And Mephibosheth, grandson of your master, will always eat at my table." (Now Ziba had fifteen sons and twenty servants.)

If you study history, you will find that when a different family took over the kingship, the new family usually destroyed the entire family of the dethroned king. They killed the king and then killed anyone who might have a claim to the throne through family lines.

In a typical situation, that's what would have happened when David became king. Jonathan and Saul had been killed in battle

(Saul actually took his own life after being wounded). When David became king, he could have issued the decree to kill all of Saul's surviving relatives—anyone who might later make a claim to the throne. He even had good reason to do this, knowing how Saul had chased him all over the country trying to kill him.

But because of the friendship he had with Jonathan, David sought out Saul's relatives to bless them, not harm them. He asked, "Is there anyone of the house of Saul to whom I can show God's kindness?" (2 Sam. 9:3).

Ziba, a servant of the household of Saul, told David that Mephibosheth was hiding in the house of Makir because he was afraid he would be destroyed. But David calmed his fears, saying, "Don't be afraid, for I will surely show you kindness for the sake of your father Jonathan. I will restore to you all the land that belonged to your grandfather Saul, and you will always eat at my table" (v. 7).

Mephibosheth went to live in the palace. Instead of being killed, he was honored and provided for. Against all precedents and rules, the grandson of the dethroned king was invited to live in the king's palace.

Because of the friendship David had with Jonathan, Mephibosheth ate at the king's table and was treated like royalty. King David even ordered that someone else work his land, take care of his crops and stock, and bring him all the revenue. (And people say friendships aren't important!)

Because Jonathan was a true friend in the face of every kind of obstacle, his descendent was blessed and ate in the house of the king. The friendships you develop in life can help *your* children to walk in blessings that others might not enjoy. And because we are friends with the King of kings, our family can eat the good of the land!

Thank God for True Friends!

Friendship is important. I thank God for the friendships I have. I thank God for the people who have stood by me through the years. I will stand with them too. You see, when people stand with you as true friends, you are willing to stand with them.

A little boy wrote the following essay on friendship:

What My Dog Means to Me

My dog means someone nice and quiet to be with.

He does not say do, like my mother.

He does not say don't, like my father.

He does not say stop, like my big brother.

My dog Spot and I just sit quietly together,

and I like him and he likes me.

(And that's why he's my best friend.)

There's a lot of truth in those few little lines. Sometimes the best thing a friend can do is just be there. When the enemy is attacking you, you don't need someone to speak harshly to you or give you a list of all the things you need to do. No, you need someone to minister the love of God to you, to sit through the night with you, to listen to you. And that's what true friends will do.

Having a friend will fulfill the need of having someone believe in you. Every individual who is alive today has a desire to be needed. And when you have a true friend, that desire is always fulfilled. The Bible tells us that two are better than one.

ECCLESIASTES 4:9-12

9 Two are better than one, because they have a good return for their work:

10 If one falls down, his friend can help him up. But pity the man who falls and has no one to help him up!

11 Also, if two lie down together, they will keep warm. But how can one keep warm alone?

12 Though one may be overpowered, two can defend themselves. A cord of three strands is not quickly broken.

The *Contemporary English Version* says it this way, "*You are better off to have a friend than to be all alone, because then you will get more enjoyment out of what you earn. If you fall, your friend can help you up. But if you fall without having a friend nearby, you are really in trouble. If you sleep alone, you won't have anyone to keep you warm on a cold night. Someone might be able to beat up one of you, but not both of you. As the saying goes, 'A rope made from three strands of cord is hard to break.'*"

A true friend will be there for you in the good times and the bad. A true friend will be there to help defend you in the hour of accusation. A true friend will be there for you no matter what. David and Jonathan give us this picture of true friendship—the kind of relationship, fellowship, and friendship we need to build with our fellow Christians.

CHAPTER TEN

Relationship Lessons We Can Learn From Paul

In the previous chapters, we've examined the elements of healthy relationships, the marriage relationship, and the relationships we have with our relatives. We've studied the covenant relationship that Abraham had with God. And we've studied the value of having godly friends, looking in some detail at the friendship of David and Jonathan.

Now let's look at the Apostle Paul's life and learn from the relationships he maintained.

The Apostle Paul accomplished more for the cause of Christ than any other person in his lifetime. And he didn't try to be a "lone ranger." He concentrated on building relationships. He often submitted himself in relationships with his peers in ministry, and he always had a team or partner traveling with him.

Being part of a team, having a base of support, is invaluable to any endeavor. No one can be successful in this life as a lone ranger. We need each other and the support that comes from strong relationships.

William Carey of England knew the value of strong relationships. He knew the importance of having friends who would support him in his endeavors.

Carey was ordained in August of 1786. During a ministers' meeting that year, Carey suggested that Jesus' command to His disciples "to teach all nations" was still in effect. Mr. Ryland, the meeting chairman, rebuked him and accused him of being an enthusiast!

Carey was greatly embarrassed. His fellow ministers treated his ideas as impractical. But that same year he met Thomas Potts, who had been in America, seen the need for missionary work, and supported Carey in his vision.

Carey began to realize that his dreams would never be fulfilled if he worked on his own. In time, God brought other people who encouraged and helped him. One day in 1793, Carey and some friends were discussing the need for foreign missions. Andrew Fuller, a fellow minister who was at that gathering, recalled, "We saw there was a gold mine in India, but it was as deep as the center of the earth." Fuller asked who would venture to explore that mine. Carey spoke up and addressed his friends: "I will venture to go down, but remember that you must hold the ropes."

By "holding the ropes," Carey meant consistently praying for him, financially supporting him, and regularly communicating on his behalf with the churches in England. His friends agreed.

Carey went to India—and made possible the translation of the Bible into numerous languages. As a direct consequence of Carey's work, the first Evangelical mission agency was created in 1792. Many have called Carey the father of modern missions, but he saw his relationship with his supporters in England as a brotherhood. He traveled to India, but he knew he was only able to accomplish what he did because of his partners back in England who were "holding the rope."

You see, it's important to have strong relationships and godly friendships. It's important to have someone "hold the rope" for you.

Others 'Held the Rope' for Paul

This account reminds me of the time the Apostle Paul was let down over the city walls in a basket by believers with whom he had a relationship. Paul had friends who helped him in ministry on several occasions. On one such occasion, his friends actually saved his life by holding a *literal* rope!

ACTS 9:22–25

22 Yet Saul grew more and more powerful and baffled the Jews living in Damascus by proving that Jesus is the Christ.

23 After many days had gone by, the Jews conspired to kill him,

24 but Saul learned of their plan. Day and night they kept close watch on the city gates in order to kill him.

25 But his followers took him by night and lowered him in a basket through an opening in the wall.

If it hadn't been for Paul's friends holding the rope, he wouldn't have lived to accomplish all that he did for God. Relationships are important!

It's tough to go through something by yourself. But when you know someone's "holding the rope" for you and supporting you, the tough times are a little easier to handle. It's easier to tackle a problem when you know you're not alone.

Paul's life gives us insight into the importance of relationships. Paul himself recognized the value of relationships—he concentrated on building relationships.

Paul and Barnabas

The story of Paul and Barnabas gives us another good Bible example of a godly relationship.

After his conversion, Paul returned to Jerusalem only to be shunned and rejected. The Christians didn't accept him because they didn't trust him. He was the one who previously had been putting them to death!

But one day a man named Barnabas befriended Paul, took him in, and personally escorted him to Peter, James, and the other elders in Jerusalem. Soon all the other believers welcomed Paul into their fellowship and the ministry.

Barnabas had a knack for seeing both the need and the potential of the people he met. He saw Paul's potential, not his past. And Paul was grateful to him for that. In time, Paul chose Barnabas to become his close friend and also his ministry partner. Together they traveled far and wide preaching the Gospel. And Barnabas didn't even mind when Paul surpassed him and became his leader, because Barnabas continued to support Paul for the sake of the Gospel.

Even though Barnabas had been the one who brought Paul in and introduced him to all the elders of the Church, Paul eventually became the one in charge. But to Barnabas, who was in charge wasn't important. What mattered was the relationship and their ability to do great things together for God.

Being overly concerned about who's in charge is one thing that hinders many people and churches from reaching their potential in God's Kingdom and in the local community. In many churches, businesses, and organizations, much more could be accomplished if people would stop worrying about who was going to get the credit.

See the Potential, Not the Past

Barnabas' relationship with Paul shows us several things. *First*, it shows us that encouraging one another is very valuable. *Second*, it's of great benefit to have someone who believes in you. *Third*, it's vital for believers to get involved in building relationships with each other. And, *fourth*, it's important to look at people the same way God looks at them.

Instead of thinking the worst about people based on the way they look or talk, or based upon their past, start seeing people the way God sees them. Instead of telling their story, saying, "Did you hear what So-and-so did," let's do what the Bible says. Galatians 6:1 says, *"Brothers, if someone is caught in a sin, YOU WHO ARE SPIRITUAL SHOULD RESTORE HIM GENTLY. But watch yourself, or you also may be tempted."*

Lessons to Learn From Paul

The following are some key lessons on relationships that we can learn from the Apostle Paul.

One lesson we can learn is this: In relationships, always try to have one friend who will believe in you and encourage you no matter what happens. (Barnabas believed in Paul and encouraged him when no one else did.)

Another key lesson is this: Relationships can save your life. (Remember, some people who had a relationship with Paul let him down in a basket over the wall in Damascus and saved his life.)

As a side thought, I often wonder if Paul had lived in our day and had been like some Christians I know, whether he would have lived to accomplish what he did. If he were like some Christians today, he would have been foolish and said, "Bless God, I can make it on my own. I don't need anyone; I'll just believe God." Notice that the man who wrote more about faith than anyone else in the whole New Testament knew the importance of friendships and relationships! Even as men and women of faith, we need each other if we're going to make it!

Another lesson in relationships we can learn from Paul is this: You can always get more done when a number of people join together than if everyone works separately.

Today we refer to this principle as the "law of synergy"—the principle stating that the efforts of two people working together can get more done than two people working separately on the same thing. Each person can work individually and accomplish a small amount. But imagine what all of us can do together if every Christian combined efforts and worked as one on the same project!

But we must realize that a thousand people, five hundred people, ten people, even two people, can't successfully work together unless they have established relationships with one another—unless they have confidence in one another. That's why building relationships is so important.

Members in Particular

Paul's life gives us insights into the importance of relationships, and we can learn valuable lessons from the relationship between him and Barnabas. Now let's examine the Epistles and discover other relationship principles practiced by Paul.

First, we see that Paul encouraged believers to develop strong relationships.

EPHESIANS 4:15-16 (NKJV)

15 But, speaking the truth in love, may grow up in all things into Him who is the head—Christ—

16 from whom the whole body, joined and knit together by what every joint supplies, according to the effective working by which every part does its share, causes growth of the body for the edifying of itself in love.

Ephesians 4:16 indicates that the parts of the human body have a relationship with each other because they are connected together through nerves, bones, sinews, ligaments, and so forth, and because they depend upon each other to function properly.

In the same way, the members of the Body of Christ must realize they are connected with each other and dependent upon each other. Believers must build relationships with each other so they can experience the value of one another.

And if someone else has a leadership position and you don't, you still need to be connected to the Body. Why? The leader needs you to fulfill your role and do your part for the project to be successful, just as the head on a human body depends upon each member of that body to function properly.

In the natural, you wouldn't be able to walk very well if the ligaments in your knee decided they didn't want to work anymore. If the knee were to say, "Well, I'm not the head, so I'm not going to do anything today," you wouldn't get very far!

Everyone in the Body of Christ has a part to play and a role to fulfill. No individual part is better or more important than another. When every part works together, the job gets done!

The Importance of Love

In studying Paul's life, we find that he had many divinely ordained relationships. His whole ministry was filled with people with whom he had relationships—godly people who brought a "supply of the Spirit" to him and encouraged him.

From Paul's writings, we can also see that he was constantly encouraging, comforting, and exhorting other believers. In many of his Epistles, Paul named some of his coworkers and others with whom he had developed a relationship. These were men and women who helped him carry out his vision.

Another lesson we learn from Paul concerning relationships is the importance of walking in love. Paul knew that love is the key component of godly relationships. In Ephesians 4:15, he said, ". . . *speaking the truth in love, we will in all things grow up into him who is the Head, that is, Christ.*"

Charles Swindoll has said, "No amount of doctrine will replace our need for encouraging relationships built on love and understanding. Knowledge may strengthen, but relationships soften. A healthy church family has both." [1]

Paul's entire Christian life and ministry reveals the high priority that Paul placed upon relationships. As much as Paul was a Bible scholar, and as much as he advocated adherence to Bible doctrine, his life and writings indicate that he placed a high value—even a priority—on relationships.

In Philippians chapter 3, Paul indicated that a high priority must be placed upon a relationship with God and also with each other.

PHILIPPIANS 3:10, 17 (NKJV)

10 that I may know Him and the power of His resurrection, and the fellowship of His sufferings, being conformed to His death. . . .

17 Brethren, join in following my example, and note those who so walk, as you have us for a pattern.

Just as I have emphasized again and again, Paul also states that we need a relationship with God and other people. And we know that we can't have a successful relationship with anyone until we first have a relationship with God.

Multiply Your Efforts

Another thing Paul accomplished through relationships was to multiply his efforts to evangelize the world by building relationships with people who duplicated his efforts. For example, he told Timothy, his son in the faith, to do the work of an evangelist.

2 TIMOTHY 4:5 (NKJV)

5 But you be watchful in all things, endure afflictions, do the work of an evangelist, fulfill your ministry.

The men and women who have trained at RHEMA Bible Training Center and members of RHEMA Bible Church are sent out into the community and into all nations to accomplish our vision of bringing hope, help, and healing to the world! That is the vision God gave me, but I couldn't accomplish it without the relationships I have built and without the people who are sent to the world to carry out the vision.

The Power in Relationships

Let's take to heart these important lessons from the Apostle Paul. Let's make the decision to join together with other members of the Body of Christ as we take our place in the Body. Let's make the decision to walk in love and make relationships a priority in our life. Let's realize that relationships are more important than pursuing great accomplishments or success alone. We can pursue great accomplishments, but we'll never reach our goals without relationships with one another.

We have also learned that in order to have strong relationships, we must take a personal interest in each other. As you read the writings of Paul, you can see that he took a personal interest in the lives of other people. We need to be personally interested in one another, and we do this by forming and maintaining relationships.

There is power available through strong relationships. Remember the illustration of the sticks? An individual stick is easy to break, but a bundle of individual sticks banded together is much stronger and difficult to break.

When you were a child, did you ever play the game "Red Rover"? Forming two opposing teams, children lock arms with each other and then shout to the other team, "Red Rover, Red Rover, send So-and-so right over!" The person sent over tries to break through the line of joined arms. The object of the game is to "capture" the other team members one by one by not allowing them to break through your line. Success depends on how tightly you are joined together.

As we join in relationship with fellow Christians, "holding hands" against the enemy and against the storms of life, we will form an unbreakable line. And we will be empowered to accomplish all that God has destined for us to achieve.

---

[1]Taken from *Growing Deep in the Christian Life* by Charles R. Swindoll. Copyright © 1986 by Multnomah Press, Portland, OR. Used by permission of Zondervan.

CHAPTER ELEVEN

Mending Broken Fences

Throughout this book, we've seen that the most important relationship we will ever have is our relationship with God through Jesus. We've learned why building relationships should be a top priority for believers, and we've seen that relationships are the lifeline of the believer.

We've examined the elements of healthy relationships and learned about the marriage relationship by studying Adam and Eve. We've learned how to have godly relationships with our relatives, and we've studied the covenant relationship that we can have with God. We've examined true friendship by studying David and Jonathan, and we've learned the value of having godly friends. We've studied Paul's life and learned about relationships from his example and his writings.

Lastly, I want to explain what to do when something goes wrong in a relationship. I want to study from the Word of God the godly way to restore a broken friendship as we talk about "mending broken fences."

As we've seen, the men and women of the Bible built relationships, and by reading their stories, we can learn a lot about building relationships in our own lives.

Unfortunately, in our fast-paced world, we've become accustomed to obtaining everything we want immediately. As a result, people often aren't willing to spend the time necessary to build lasting relationships. And if something goes wrong in a relationship, they either bail out or want a "quick fix."

And when it comes to maintaining our relationships, including our relationship with God, we have to make a conscious effort to maintain a healthy relationship. You see, it's great to obtain a relationship with God, but we must also make sure that we maintain it.

When cowboys take care of cattle on a ranch, sometimes they have to "ride the fences." When a cowboy "rides the fences," he takes his tools and wire with him as he rides around the property, making sure that the fences are in good condition so the cattle can't wander off and get lost. If he finds a broken strand of wire or a broken fence, he mends the fence then and there.

In the same way, we have to "ride the fences" of our relationship with God to make sure that we don't wander away from the Lord and become lost. (When I say "riding the fences," I am not referring to "straddling the fence," which implies a person is trying to take a position on both sides of an issue.)

It is also important that we continue to "ride the fences" of our human relationships, so we do not lose our relationships with one another. Most relationships are broken when someone becomes offended over something that someone else has said or done. But we must be quick to mend the relationship so it's not severed permanently.

Check Your Fences

You may already have a relationship with God, and that is wonderful. You may have become a Christian years ago. But is the relationship between you and the Lord still strong after all these years?

People who accepted Christ years ago may have allowed their "fences" to come into disrepair. These people may not be in fellowship and relationship with God as closely as they used to be or as closely as they should be.

JOHN 8:3-11

3 The teachers of the law and the Pharisees brought in a woman caught in adultery. They made her stand before the group

4 and said to Jesus, "Teacher, this woman was caught in the act of adultery.

5 In the Law Moses commanded us to stone such women. Now what do you say?"

6 They were using this question as a trap, in order to have a basis for accusing him. But Jesus bent down and started to write on the ground with his finger.

7 When they kept on questioning him, he straightened up and said to them, "If any one of you is without sin, let him be the first to throw a stone at her."

8 Again he stooped down and wrote on the ground.

9 At this, those who heard began to go away one at a time, the older ones first, until only Jesus was left, with the woman still standing there.

10 Jesus straightened up and asked her, "Woman, where are they? Has no one condemned you?"

11 "No one, sir," she said. "Then neither do I condemn you," Jesus declared. "Go now and leave your life of sin."

Here is a picture of someone who "let her fences down" and found herself away from God, and involved in a life of sin.

How many times have we unintentionally wandered away and found ourselves in a broken relationship with God because of sin? What is God's response in those situations?

Well, we know that the heart of God is to have a relationship with His people. And in John 8:3–11, we find a story showing that God wants to restore broken relationships.

In this particular account, there is no doubt that sinful actions had taken place. The woman had been caught in the very act of adultery, and Exodus 20:14 says, *"You shall not commit adultery."* This woman had broken the Law of Moses by her sexual immorality, and according to the Law of Moses, she deserved to be put to death.

LEVITICUS 20:10

10 "'If a man commits adultery with another man's wife—with the wife of his neighbour—both the adulterer and the adulteress must be put to death.'"

No mercy or grace was to be extended to her at all. A swift and cruel punishment was her lot under the law.

You could say it this way: The fences of her relationship with God were in bad condition and allowed her to wander away from God.

The Religious Response

Let's look at the religious actions of the Pharisees and teachers of the Law.

The motive of the religious leaders for bringing this woman was to trap Jesus into saying something that was contradictory to the Law of Moses.

Imagine the wrath and scorn that the religious leaders expressed toward this woman. Imagine the despair that filled this woman as they dragged her along and accused her in front of Jesus!

The Pharisees were highly incensed that Jesus forgave people of their sin and showed mercy and grace. The religious people wanted judgment. And there is no wrath like religious fury! It stops at nothing to get what it thinks is right, even if it's contrary to what God's Word says about grace, mercy, and restoration.

Religion is consumed with what is "right" and does not care about the restoration of mankind. Religious fury does not rest until vengeance has been issued upon the object found in violation of its rules. Religion condemns the individuals that fail to live up to its impossible demands. Holy wars and crusades have even been fought in the name of religion!

Religion does not care about the feelings or well-being of a person. It only cares about what the rules say—even when the rules are contrary to the Word or nature of God. (Religious tradition is dangerous ground to base your life upon if the traditions are contrary to the Word of God.)

The religious leaders in John chapter 8 didn't care about the woman. They cared more about their doctrine! (Actually, what they *really* cared about was the fact that Jesus' teaching challenged their authority.)

Notice that the religious leaders took only the woman to Jesus. Why didn't they also take the man to Jesus? The fact that the religious leaders took only the woman to Jesus revealed that they did not act with the right motives. If they'd really been concerned about their *law* and doctrine, they would have presented the man to Jesus too. Leviticus 20:10 says both the adulterer and the adulteress must be put to death.

The Pharisees acted as though they wanted justice, but when Jesus showed them real justice, they took off. Jesus showed them what real justice was when He said: "... *'If any one of you is without sin, let him be the first to throw a stone at her'*" (John 8:7). The religious leaders were guilty of breaking the law themselves, and thus were unqualified to deal with this situation.

All some people want to do is talk about Christians who have made mistakes. But the Word of God says that those who are spiritual should pray and restore that fallen brother or sister (Gal. 6:1). Before we start talking about what someone else has done, we should think about our own mistakes. If it weren't for the mercy and grace of God, we'd all be in a mess!

The Righteous Response

We've seen the *religious* actions of the Pharisees and teachers of the Law. Now let's look at the *righteous* actions of Jesus.

First, Jesus confronted the religious leaders with their own actions. Second, He did not condemn the woman, but rather restored her relationship with God. Although Jesus didn't condemn her, notice that He didn't overlook her offense as if it had never happened. He acknowledged that it was there, but he told her to "sin no more." In other words, "Don't break your relationship with God again."

Jesus brought back into focus what was really important—the restoration of the woman's relationship with God. This whole story reveals God's desire to have and maintain a relationship with mankind.

Confession Is Good for the Relationship

God desires to have a maintained relationship with us. But you and I are the ones who are responsible for maintaining the relationship. It's not God's responsibility. He's already done all He needs to do to make a way for us to have a relationship with Him. If we're going to have a relationship with God, we must spend time with Him. We have to communicate with Him and make the decision and effort to stay in right standing with Him.

How do we maintain our relationship with Him and stay in right standing with Him? How do we mend the broken fences of our relationship if we've wandered from Him? Let's look at His Word and find out.

1 JOHN 1:9

9 If we confess our sins, he is faithful and just and will forgive us our sins and purify us from all unrighteousness.

The *New Century Version* of this verse says, *"But if we confess our sins, he will forgive our sins, because we can trust God to do what is right. He will cleanse us from all the wrongs we have done."*

God's Word translation says, *"God is faithful and reliable. If we confess our sins, he forgives them and cleanses us from everything we've done wrong."*

The Book of First John was not written to sinners, but to the Church—to Christians. So this scripture is God's Word to us! He is telling us what to do to restore and continue to maintain the relationship we have with Him.

First John 1:9 says, *"If we confess our sins, he is faithful and just and will forgive us our sins and purify us from all unrighteousness."* When it says, "confess," it's talking about you and God. You don't have to confess your sins to a person in order to be forgiven by God. This verse is talking about confessing your sins to God, saying, "God, I made a mistake. I missed it!"

The Choice Is Yours!

Notice the beginning of verse 9 says, *"IF we confess our sins. . . ."* The choice is yours—whether or not you will confess what you did or said wrong as sin. But if we want to mend the broken fences and maintain a right relationship with God, we must choose to do this.

We can't rationalize our mistake by saying, "Well, it's really not *that* bad." Or, "So-and-so got away with it." No, the easiest way to maintain a relationship with God is for you to be willing to say, "God, I messed up. Forgive me." (Some people choose not to ask for forgiveness, and do not maintain their relationship with God.)

We must confess, or acknowledge, our sin to God and ask Him to forgive us and cleanse us from any unrighteousness. Our part is to confess our sin. When we do our part, God does His part. What's His part? God forgives and restores. In effect, He says to you what Jesus said to the woman in John chapter 8: "Yes, you messed up, but I don't condemn you. Now don't do it anymore."

You see, God is faithful and just (1 John 1:9), and He always keeps His Word. And His Word says that when we confess, He forgives and restores!

Parents, Keep Your Word

As a side note to parents, let me say that one reason some parents have trouble with their children is because the parents aren't being just. Unjust parents change the rules in the middle of the game, so to speak. In other words, they don't keep their word. That will provoke children to wrath, which is unbiblical according to Ephesians 6:4.

Parents, if you're going to change the rules, then you better have a meeting with your children and let them know which rules have been changed.

Let me warn you, it's very difficult to change the rules once the game has started. So before you set the rules of the house, spend some time thinking and praying. *Then* set your rules. And once you put your word out to your children, be sure to keep it.

God's Word Is His Bond

When it comes to our Heavenly Father, we can count on Him to do what He said He would do! Being faithful and just is part of God's character, and God will always act according to His character.

God's Word reveals His character to us. God will always do what His Word has promised, because God is not a man that He should lie (Num. 23:19). So we can trust God and count on Him to do what He says. And His Word says that if we confess our sins, He will forgive us and cleanse us from all unrighteousness (1 John 1:9).

Second Peter 3:9 says, *"The Lord is not slow in keeping his promise, as some understand slowness. He is patient with you, not wanting anyone to perish, but everyone to come to repentance."*

You can mend the broken fences in your relationship with God. God is patient and kind. He will forgive you, restore your relationship with Him, and make everything brand-new!

Time to Take Inventory

Today is the day for you to "ride the fence" on your relationship with God and on the other relationships in your life. Are the fences of your relationships in good condition, or do they need to be repaired?

You can mend the broken fences, the broken relationships, in your life today. If it's your relationship with God that needs mending, simply do what First John 1: 9 says. God will forgive you, restore your relationship with Him, and make everything brand-new. He will also help you mend the broken relationship you may have with a loved one or friend.

You may not have committed adultery like the woman in John chapter 8; maybe you haven't committed any blatant sin.

Perhaps it's just that your fences aren't as strong as they used to be or as they should be. Maybe your relationship isn't completely broken, but it's been weakening and you need to mend some things. Today is the day to say, "Lord, forgive me. Help me because I'm headed down the wrong road."

In natural things, it's important to take inventory of our lives on a regular basis and see where we are. Storeowners take "inventory" regularly to measure their success. They ask, "Are we selling enough product? Do we have too much product on hand? Do we have a checks-and-balances system in such-and-such area? Are we meeting our budget? What can we do to improve?"

Today is the day to take an inventory of your life. Ask yourself, "Am I maintaining a close relationship with God? Am I maintaining a strong relationship with my spouse and family? And am I maintaining a godly relationship with my brothers and sisters in the Lord? What can I do to improve my relationships?" If you find that there are some weaknesses or some broken strands in your relationships, this is the day to mend them.

Mending broken fences is a simple message, but it is vitally important to our relationship with God and our relationships with our brothers and sisters in the Lord.

Whatever area of relationships you may be struggling with, I pray you receive the help and wisdom you need to be victorious. If there is a particular kind of relationship that you need to build or strengthen in your life, I pray you will make the decision today to do so. I pray that you will then take the godly principles you've read in this book and apply them to those relationships.

And I pray that we all make whatever adjustments need to be made in order for us to establish and maintain healthy, strong, and prosperous relationships with God and with others. When our relationships with God and with others are strong, we can reach our potential and achieve all that God has destined us to accomplish!

Why should you consider attending

Rhema
Bible Training College?

Rhema Word Partner Club

WORKING *together* TO REACH THE WORLD!

WPC

People. Power. Purpose.

Have you ever dropped a stone into water? Small waves rise up at the point of impact and travel in all directions. It's called a ripple effect. That's the kind of impact Christians are meant to have in this world—the kind of impact that the Rhema family is producing in the earth today.

The Rhema Word Partner Club links Christians with a shared interest in reaching people with the Gospel and the message of faith in God.

Together we are reaching across generations, cultures, and nations to spread the Good News of Jesus Christ to every corner of the earth.

To join us in reaching the world,
visit **www.rhema.org/wpc** or call **1-866-312-0972**.

Always on.

For the latest news and information on products, media, podcasts, study resources, and special offers, visit us online 24 hours a day.

www.rhema.org

Free Subscription!

Call now to receive a free subscription to *The Word of Faith* magazine from Kenneth Hagin Ministries. Receive encouragement and spiritual refreshment from . . .

- *Faith-building articles from Kenneth W. Hagin, Lynette Hagin, Craig W. Hagin, and others*
- *"Timeless Teaching" from the archives of Kenneth E. Hagin*
- *Feature articles on prayer and healing*
- *Testimonies of salvation, healing, and deliverance*
- *Children's activity page*
- *Updates on Rhema Bible Training College, Rhema Bible Church, and other outreaches of Kenneth Hagin Ministries*

Subscribe today for your free *Word of Faith*!

1-888-28-FAITH (1-888-283-2484)

www.rhema.org/wof

OFFER CODE—BKORD:WF